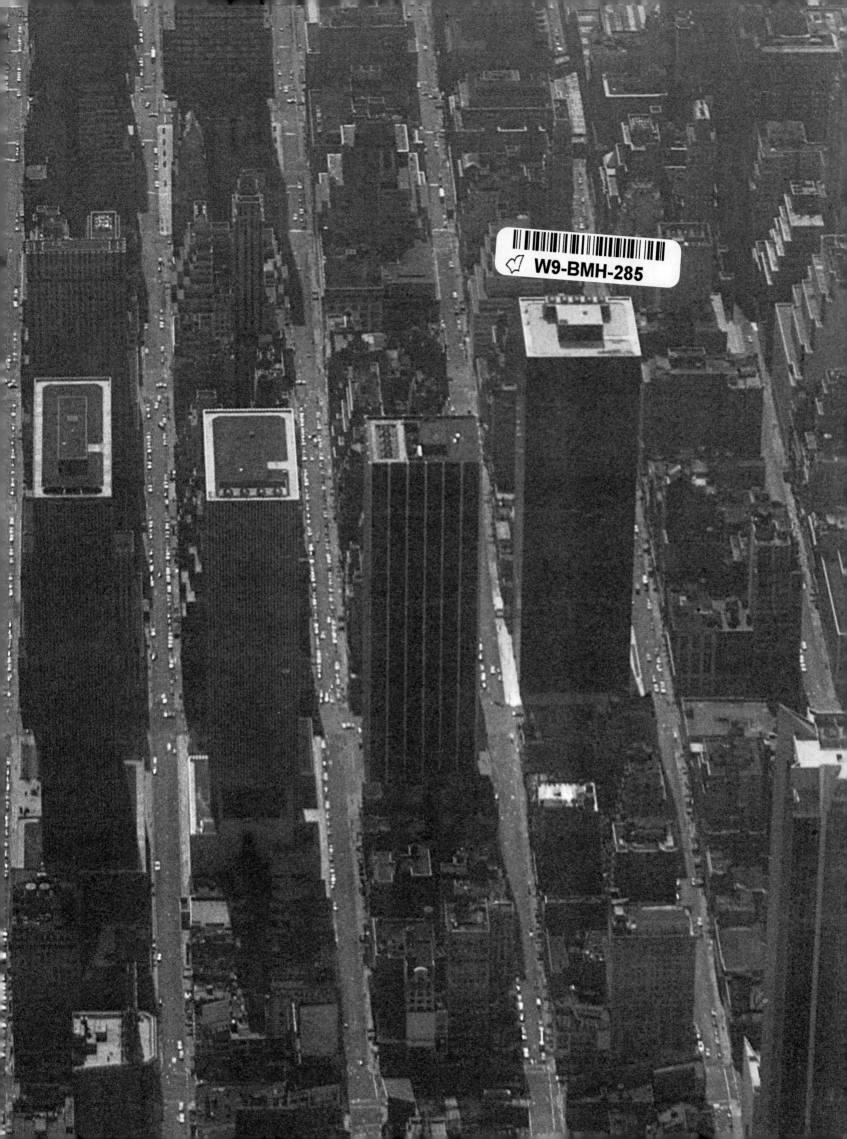

NEW YORK

By Anthony Burgess
and the Editors of Time-Life Books

With Photographs by
Dan Budnik
Enrico Ferorelli
Leonard Freed
Chester Higgins
Jay Maisel

THE GREAT CITIES · TIME-LIFE BOOKS · AMSTERDAM

The Author: Anthony Burgess was born in Manchester, England, in 1917 and educated there, chiefly by Catholic priests but also by secular professors at Manchester University. He wanted to be a musician and also a newspaper cartoonist but became a teacher instead—both in England and in the dwindling British Colonial Empire. Invalided home from Borneo, he became a full-time writer. Since 1956 he has published more than 30 books. Of these *A Clockwork Orange*, filmed in 1971, has been the greatest popular success. Burgess composes music and his third symphony was performed in Iowa. He knows New York City well, having taught at Columbia University and City College, as well as at near-by Princeton.

Editor: Dale Brown
Design Consultant: Louis Klein
Picture Editor: Pamela Marke
Assistant Picture Editor: Anne Angus

Editorial Staff for New York
Deputy Editor: Christopher Farman
Text Editor: Jim Hicks
Designer: Graham Davis
Staff Writers: Mike Brown, Deborah Thompson
Text Researchers: Susie Dawson, Vanessa Kramer
Design Assistant: Shirin Patel

Editorial Production for the Series
Art Department: Julia West
Editorial Department: Ellen Brush, Jan Piggott,
Betty H. Weatherley
Picture Department: Cathy Doxat-Pratt, Thelma Gilbert,
Christine Hinze

The captions and the text of the picture essays were written by the staff of TIME-LIFE Books.

Valuable assistance was given in the preparation of this volume by Peggy Bushong, Neil Kagan, Dolores Littles, Mary Kay Moran, Mel Scott, TIME-LIFE Books, New York.

Published by TIME-LIFE International (Nederland) B.V. Ottho Heldringstraat 5, Amsterdam 10 18.

Cover: New York's electric dynamism is captured in an interpretative photograph of the midtown area, with the Empire State Building glowing at its centre. To achieve the light-streaked effect, the photographer elevated his tripod while making a time-exposure.

First end paper: A hazy afternoon sun shines on the grid-patterned cross-town streets of mid-Manhattan, running ruler-straight between the regiments of skyscrapers.

Last end paper: Gaunt warehouses with bricked-up windows stand blank and silent near Manhattan's West Side waterfront.

Contents

I

The Real New York

My problem is, I think, mainly a stylistic one: *how* to write about New York City. The only verse-form that *seems* proper—free yet biblical, lyrical yet catalogic—was long ago pre-empted by the New York poet Walt Whitman to express the surging vigour of 19th-Century America; besides, this is a prose age. To use prose, however, is to be seduced, unless I keep my head, into echoing the overblown hyperbole of Madison Avenue, since the only alternative seems to be the chill monody of statistics. But this is a lover's book, so I shall risk the purple; and since this lover is also an Englishman, I shall blush occasionally at exhibiting too much emotion and so attempt the detached manner of a Gibbon.

I propose, then, to be as honest as it is possible for a lover to be; and I will be *very* honest at the outset, foregoing the usual authorial stance of calm and competence. I have written and published more than 30 books, but I have approached none of them with the fear and trembling I bring to my present task.

My first impressions of New York were emotive and very limited, as befits a slowly dawning love affair. When I was a boy in Manchester, my image of America was inevitably gained from the movies I saw. In the 1920s, my great epoch of movie-going, I was dealt a dumb monochrome America consisting of five provinces: the Wild West, Southern California, Chicago, some generic university town and New York. New York itself was reduced to one locale—the island of Manhattan—and the city's other four boroughs must forgive me if I concentrate in this first chapter on the source and focus of so much of my childhood fantasy. Manhattan was chiefly skyscrapers, easy for a youngster to draw, and no other place in the world expressed itself in such simple hieroglyphs. Doodling for me was very often just drawing a sort of Manhattan skyline. I knew New York: it lay in my pencil box.

But then the talking-films arrived and for a time I no longer knew it. The growling or booming or scratchy dissonances of these early movies disclosed to the British that America had a different sound from England, and that the sound of New York was particularly and horribly alien. The city was further diminished to a single street—Broadway—and was inhabited exclusively by wisecracking, hardboiled chorines and desperate song-and-dance men. But as the talkies talked more, and sang and danced less, New York grew familiar again and even began to provide me with the basic parameters of metropolitan life. There was jungle toughness, but also

Hardened to the hazardous ways of his world, a New York City cab driver bites on the stump of his cigar while waiting for a traffic light to change. About 12,000 licensed cabs, painted yellow for visibility, cruise the city's streets, their drivers as willing to listen to their passengers' troubles as to tell their own.

sophistication, glamour, chic, wit. I had not yet visited London, although I assumed that in a London restaurant you waited for a table behind a velvet rope and were eventually allotted one by somebody Latin called the "maiter dee". You surely drank highballs in London and it was not to be doubted that ice clinked in everything. ("Ice?" a London barman said to me when I at last reached a London bar. "Where would I get ice from on a day like this?") London lawyers, I supposed, looked like Melvyn Douglas, had offices in penthouses and in court said, "Your witness." I thought of London's Underground as similar to the New York Subway and, when I first used it, was astonished at its actually being so clean and orderly.

The time came when New York displayed itself to me through literature, but a time later still showed how inadequate that literature was. No writer I know of has ever succeeded in exhibiting the whole panorama. Most writers on New York have found it easier to create a city of their own than to reproduce the reality. As a result, the images of New York recorded in the popular arts seemed—and still seem—truer than those in books.

In the clichéd imaginings of the Old World the New World is chiefly New York—restless, febrile, neurotic, brutal, endlessly creative, endlessly destructive, prizing the new for novelty's sake, bizarre in its cultural and racial variety; Irish cops with night-sticks, Jewish impresarios with cigars, slums and penthouses, champagne air in a killing climate, perpetual decay and perpetual rebirth. But if the reality, when we meet it at last, shows how impotent all art must be when faced with the task of fixing the city on paper or even film, it also demonstrates that we who are born to the Old are not entirely wrong in believing that anything is possible to the New. If you imagine something that Old logic says cannot exist—say, cabbage stewed in double cream and saffron, or a one-legged black Armenian poetess whose father's name was O'Shaughnessy—you are likely to find it, or at least go searching for it, in New York.

A 19th-Century print suggests how the tree-clad tip of Manhattan island looked to its discoverer, Henry Hudson, in 1609. His ship, the Half Moon, lies to the left. The English navigator, on a voyage of exploration for the Dutch East India Company, was the first to bring back to Europe a full account of the landlocked harbour and its rich hinterland.

Away from the city, I sometimes wonder whether I am remembering a dream or an actuality. Were there really three men playing Bach on clarinets on Broadway near 96th Street, while a mugged man's blood drained unheeded into the gutter? Perhaps it was only two clarinettists and perhaps there was not much blood. I am pretty certain that, coming home from a party at four in the morning, I found a bearded thug following me down Columbus Avenue, running when I ran, catching up to say that he disagreed with something I had written on the poetry of Andrew Marvell. Speech and appearance are not necessarily, as they are in London, a guide to the man within. Nor is trade identifiable with vocation: in a new world a man is always trying to be a new man. An immigration officer who processed me at Kennedy Airport sent me the typescript of a highly experimental novel; I once got a taxi-driver a Broadway audition, if not a role. There is a phantasmal quality about New York's image, appropriate to a water city. It is as if events are borne along on a swift tide.

My uneasiness about how to describe New York is matched by a certain guilt about the continuing honeymoon quality of my relationship to it, or her (Ezra Pound described the city as "a maid with no breasts . . . slender as a silver reed"). I have never shivered on Ellis Island with an immigrant's thin overcoat and cardboard suitcase, nor been desperate over the rent of a cold-water flat, nor even, as yet, been soundly mugged. My first visit to New York came when I was mature and already had something of a small literary reputation, and I arrived to warmth and the flesh-and-blood continuation of friendships already begun by letter.

I found the place kinder and softer-spoken than the movies had taught me to expect. I was prepared for toughness and rudeness but got little of either, perhaps because of my own cautious politeness. I was lucky in my first taxi-driver, who kindly confided that the British, though effete, had various moderately fine gentlemanly qualities. I stayed at the Algonquin,

Where the first Dutch settlement once stood, the skyscrapers that crowd Manhattan's narrow southern point now rise hundreds of feet into the air. Seen over the broad stern of a departing Staten Island ferry, they mark out Manhattan from New Jersey (left) and the shores of Brooklyn (right) stretching north-eastwards towards Queens.

The Faces of the City

You can believe there is such a thing as a typical New Yorker—until you get to New York. But a day or two of observation suffices to prove the inhabitants' infinite variety.

Throughout its history the city has impressed observers by the endless mixture—racial, social, political, cultural—of its population, drawn continually from every country of the world and from every corner of the United States. For, if a happy-shirted Puerto Rican (top right) is a typical New Yorker, so is a melancholy black from Harlem (bottom row, second from right); so is a bow-tied art-lover at a smart party (same row)—or for that matter, any of the others in this photographic mosaic. From such a wealth of types the unique gift of New York to its people is conjured: the freedom and the opportunity to be fully and vividly themselves. And it is one of the secrets of the lasting spell of the city that there are as many real New Yorkers as there are people in New York.

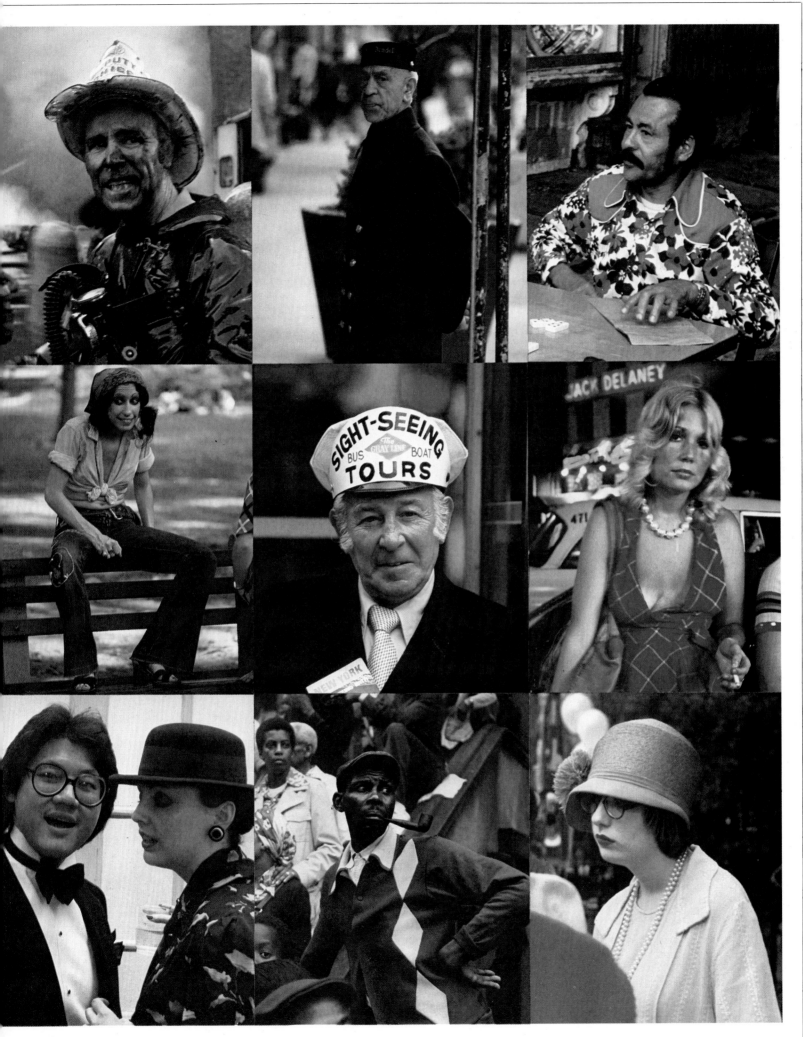

just off Fifth Avenue, which is fond of writers and has a cosy British ambience. Until recently it was obligatory to wear a necktie in the Blue Bar.

The time was to come when I should have an apartment of my own on the West Side or commute from New Jersey, undergo the black man's hate, face the enmity of the young, be involved in the tooth-and-claw life of the Broadway theatre. But I have always felt at home in New York, more so than in London. In New York City the essential human condition is not masked, as in England, by an intricate class structure; your accent is not held very much against you; your concern with making a living is everybody's concern. The towering solidity of the architecture is one thing; the insubstantiality of a man's place in the stone canyons is quite another. New York is a displaced persons' camp. I—a writer always in exile, an Englishman whose grandmother was a Finnegan from Tipperary, a sort of medievalist in a mechanized world—am a paradigm of displacement. New York has to be my preferred city.

I remain, however, whether I like it or not, a product of British history, disposed to look for Englishry in a city whose *lingua franca* is a kind of English, and whose history in part belongs to the dead Empire of which I was once a subject. If the Italian, Giovanni da Verrazano, was the first explorer to sight the terrain in 1524, the Englishman, Henry Hudson, was the first, almost a century later, to sail into its harbour, pressing up the tidal river that now bears his name, searching—like all explorers of the Renaissance—for a westward route to the Indian spicelands. I carry a mild traditional resentment of Dutch enterprise and aggression, and find it hard to forgive Hudson for navigating on behalf of the Dutch East India Company, instead of Britain's King James I. It was Hudson's report of a great sheltered harbour and an infinitude of potential farmland that brought the colonists from Old to New Netherland, and led Peter Minuit, director-general of what was to become not only New York but also Connecticut, New Jersey and Long Island, to that mad purchase of Manhattan from the Algonquin Indians—the unassessable wealth of the future for a few trinkets.

But of course New York—or rather New Amsterdam—had to be British sooner or later. There was the need to secure geographical continuity between the existing British colonies in North America, and New Amsterdam was an interrupting alien fist. In the 1660s Britain and Holland were great maritime competitors. If a Dutch fleet could sail up the Thames, a British one could sail up the Hudson. In 1664 the city was taken without the firing of a single shot and renamed not for Old York but for James, Duke of York, King Charles II's brother. It all went so well because the Dutch preferred alien rule to the tyranny of their own one-legged governor, Peter Stuyvesant. However, that tendency to racial fusion so characteristic of the city (in spite of periodic bouts of raging xenophobia), that refusal to reproduce slavishly in the New World the nationalistic rivalries of the Old, forbade that New York be a mere colony for very long. Dutch and

A daring construction worker high above Manhattan works on the steel skeleton of the towering Empire State Building as construction of the 102-storey structure nears completion in 1931. New York's tallest building for 40 years, the Empire State was superseded in 1971 by the twin towers of the World Trade Center, each 110 storeys tall.

English—best thought of in, say, 1690 as just "New Yorkers"—joined amicably in resenting the autocracy of the British Crown. It has never been easy to think of royal New York; to enter Manhattan even now is to board a kind of pirate ship. Was not Captain Kidd one of the city's leading citizens, a respected pewholder in the Trinity Church he helped to build?

Commercial sharpness, hatred of bureaucracy, a somewhat shady spirit of independence, a tolerance of freebooting, an ethical easiness unthinkable in New England—these attributes appeal to the independent artist in me if not to the stern Englishman. And it is very much the writer in me who is stirred by the story of John Peter Zenger (neither Dutch nor English, but a German turned good New Yorker), publisher and editor of the *New York Weekly-Journal*. In the 1730s it was he who made the first American stand for the freedom of the Press by publishing scathing attacks on the colonial administration. Jailed for libel, he fought like a true New Yorker, continuing to edit the *Journal* from his cell. Powerful commercial interests chafing at British rule gave Zenger their support and the brilliant Philadelphia lawyer, Andrew Hamilton, championed him in the courts, prevailing on the jury to ignore the judge's directive and return a defiant verdict of Not Guilty.

In 1774, the local Sons of Liberty, inspired by the example of their fellow Patriots in Boston, staged their own "tea party"; and the provincial governor, Cadwallader Colden, reported to London: "The present political zeal and phrenzy is almost entirely confined to the City of New-York." It is said that the first blood of the fight for independence was spilt in this city—in January, 1775, when one of the Sons of Liberty was killed by a Redcoat. Here, as an Englishman, I am expected to waver in loyalty, but one of my ancestors was killed by a British soldier—in the Peterloo Massacre of 1819, when a protest meeting of Manchester workers was cut down by Hussars. My resentment of that makes me a kind of New Yorker.

Is there any Englishry left in the city? There are certainly Englishmen who, immigrants as much as the Poles and the Puerto Ricans, are nevertheless not easy to dig out from the main mass of first-language English speakers. It is, of course, the language itself, along with a sort of English literary tradition, that stands as the only true inheritance from the land that James, Duke of York, was to rule as king and be driven from as tyrant. And that language, in its New York form, has become not merely autonomous but perhaps the major dialect of world English. Any visiting English writer feels the comparative effeteness of his own medium: it is achieved, finished, already approaching petrification, while the English of New York is always on the forge.

For the rest, the culture of England enjoys no pre-eminence in this city. English pubs, taverns and eating-houses are to be found; but, like the cafés and restaurants dispensing French cuisine, they are mere oases of exotica. England has been swallowed up, as has Holland; and of Holland there are not even many linguistic memorials. If, in New York, I remain an Englishman, it is only as others remain Lithuanians and Basques. Indeed, in this city that bears so English a name, the English claim to primacy is weaker than most; for the English have a sin to expiate of which none of the other component peoples can be held guilty: that of presiding over the near-destruction of New York. It happened during the War of Independence, when there was not really very much to destroy—an agglomeration of old Dutch and new English dwellings at the southernmost tip of the island of Manhattan, with a population of 20,000 or so. Strategically, the British were right to capture New York from the American rebels. Here was the Hudson River, extending almost to Lake George, which in turn led to Lake Champlain, which emptied into the Richelieu River, which in its turn emptied into the St. Lawrence—a kind of great water-line to use as a knife for cutting the American forces in two and isolating New England. Here, too, was the island of Manhattan itself, an admirable winter barracks for the invading troops, easily protected by the Royal Navy, which was powerful, while the American Navy was non-existent.

It is a bizarre imaginative exercise to dig down and look for the naked city of the fighting of the autumn of 1776. There is General George

The tip of the 77-storey Chrysler Building climbs skywards in all its shiny Art Deco magnificence. Completed in 1930 at the height of the Depression, the building was one of the first skyscrapers to make use of metal sheathing to dynamic effect.

Washington, at dawn on September 15, on what is now 161st Street, looking south towards a small Dutch settlement called Harlem, round about 125th Street, where the British were expected to attack. There is General Sir William Howe, the British commander, planning the final dispositions of his 23,000 Redcoats and 9,000 German mercenaries. Five British frigates are at Kip's Bay, at the foot of East 34th Street, and near 89th Street and East Avenue the British are trying to silence the nine-gun American battery at Horn's Hook.

By evening, New York's defenders had succumbed to the vastly superior British forces and the following month Washington was forced to retreat across the Hudson. Six days after its capture, the city was ravaged by fire and, although the British had least to gain by destroying their valuable prize, they naturally got the blame. "Providence or some good honest fellow," gloated Washington, "has done more for us than we were disposed to do for ourselves."

A second mysterious blaze broke out in 1778 and, when the British finally marched out of New York five years later, much of it still lay in ruins. But recovery was quick. In 1785 the resurgent city became for a single heady year the capital of the American nation and the first presidential inauguration—of that great non-New Yorker George Washington—took place there. Demoted from national to state capital, New York lost even that doubtful honour in 1797. It was obviously destined to become a different kind of metropolis.

But this is to dwell on ancient wrongs and past glories, and here I am more concerned with present reality. I remember that Manchester schoolboy dreamily doodling his city of towers, for in those towers the dream and the reality meet. The architectural glamour of Manhattan derives, like many kinds of beauty, from an enforced limitation. Like Venice, it is set upon by water. The Hudson and East Rivers and Upper New York Bay seem, at first glance, to define it as a smooth-sided peninsula, but the slim knife of the Harlem River separates it from the northern mainland. Unlike Venice, however, Manhattan has a firm foundation of solid rock, essential to its architectural monoliths. To expand, it sought the air, defying the old view of power, which measured territorial greatness by the square mile, and leading us to a new science-fiction vision in which the world can be ruled from a few square yards if the superstructure is high enough. We can think of a whole nation housed in a single skyscraper, of an army mobilizing in rhythmical elevator-loads.

What sight can touch that incredible skyline, seen from Upper New York Bay or when riding in from New Jersey? And yet it is a beauty of forced compression, since Manhattan has no monopoly of skyscrapers, only a tighter line-up of them. Manhattan also has charm, if charm is the quality you find in beauty unself-conscious and uncontrived. It is the work of many

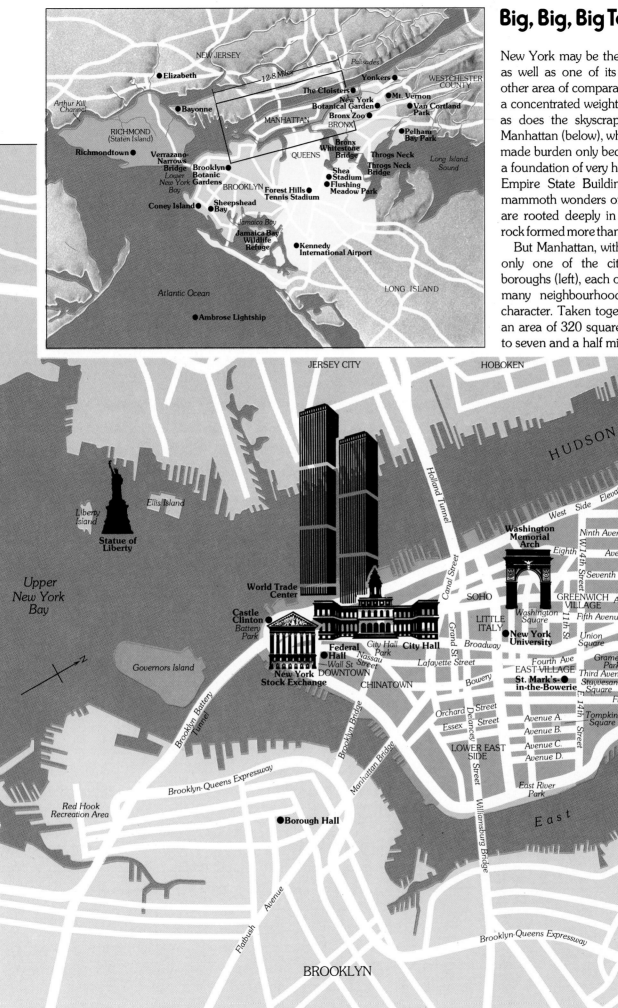

Big, Big, Big Town

New York may be the world's heaviest city, as well as one of its largest. Certainly no other area of comparable size supports such a concentrated weight of concrete and steel as does the skyscraper-jammed island of Manhattan (below), which can carry its man-made burden only because nature provided a foundation of very hard bedrock. Thus the Empire State Building and all the other mammoth wonders of modern architecture are rooted deeply in the past—planted in rock formed more than 400 million years ago.

But Manhattan, with its soaring towers, is only one of the city's five water-edged boroughs (left), each of which is made up of many neighbourhoods of varying ethnic character. Taken together, they encompass an area of 320 square miles and are home to seven and a half million people.

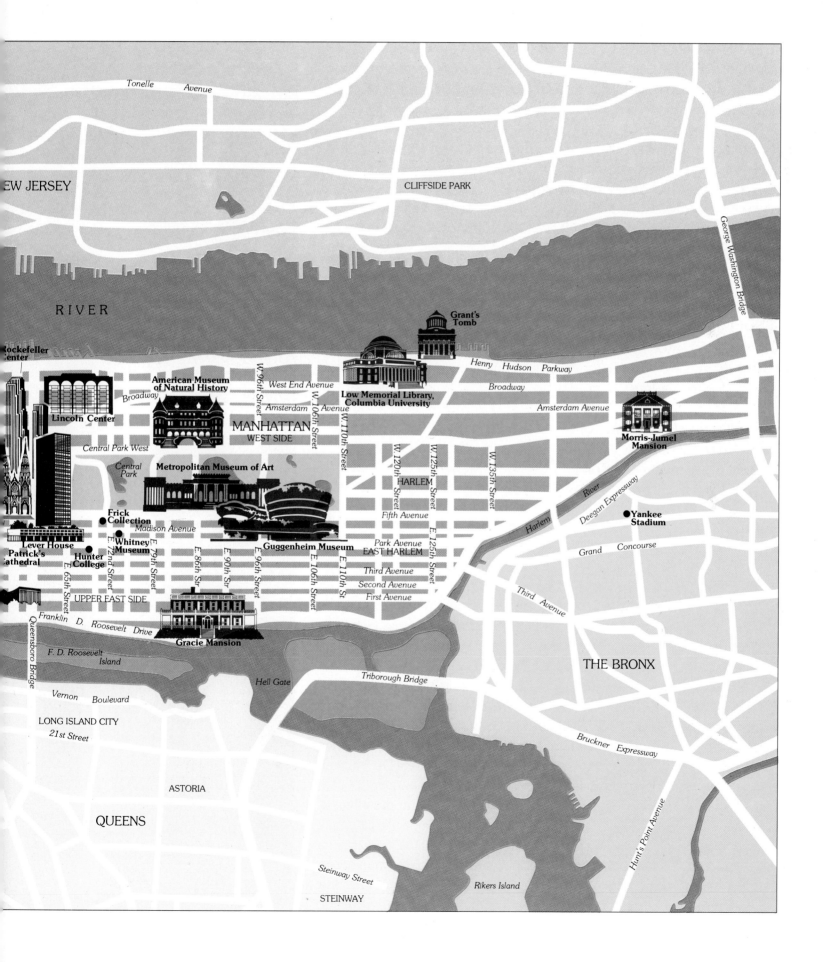

NEW JERSEY

CLIFFSIDE PARK

Tonelle Avenue

RIVER

George Washington Bridge

Grant's Tomb

Rockefeller Center

American Museum of Natural History

Low Memorial Library, Columbia University

Henry Hudson Parkway

Broadway

Lincoln Center

Broadway

W. 96th Street

West End Avenue

Amsterdam Avenue

W. 106th Street

W. 110th Street

Amsterdam Avenue

Morris-Jumel Mansion

MANHATTAN
WEST SIDE

Central Park West

Central Park

Metropolitan Museum of Art

W. 120th Street

W. 125th Street

W. 135th Street

HARLEM

Harlem River

Deegan Expressway

Frick Collection

Madison Avenue

Fifth Avenue

Yankee Stadium

Whitney Museum

Guggenheim Museum

Park Avenue
EAST HARLEM

E. 125th Street

Lever House

Hunter College

E. 72nd Street

E. 79th Street

E. 86th Str.

E. 90th Str.

E. 96th Street

E. 106th Street

E. 110th St.

Third Avenue

Grand Concourse

Patrick's Cathedral

E. 65th Street

Second Avenue

First Avenue

Third Avenue

UPPER EAST SIDE

Franklin D. Roosevelt Drive

Gracie Mansion

THE BRONX

Queensboro Bridge

F. D. Roosevelt Island

Hell Gate

Triborough Bridge

Vernon Boulevard

LONG ISLAND CITY
21st Street

Bruckner Expressway

ASTORIA

Hunt's Point Avenue

QUEENS

Steinway Street

Rikers Island

STEINWAY

architects and builders, each concerned with his own creation, each bliss-fully unconcerned with the whole. Thus every human scale is exhibited, from the squat two-storey shack to the topless tower, and it is the cramming together of so much diversity that gives Manhattan its enchantment.

The twin-towered, 110-storey World Trade Center is in the Wall Street area, but so is Captain Kidd's Trinity Church. The International Building, on a corner of the massive Rockefeller Center complex, looks across Fifth Avenue at the neo-Gothic grandeur (or is it horror?) of St. Patrick's Cathedral. Manhattan reveals its most startling aspect when one looks down from some high vantage point at Central Park, especially in spring. Its thawed blue waters and young greenery are completely surrounded by a stone army of buildings—a ragtime army made up of dwarfs and giants, looking with a kind of distracted benignity at this thing called Nature.

The skyscraper is as much to be associated with Chicago as with Man-hattan, but New York was the first to build high; and the Equitable Life Assurance Society's five-storey building, finished by Gilman, Kendall and Post in 1870, was a giant for its time. Then came William Le Baron Jenney's structural innovation: the inner iron frame, which cut out the need for massive foundations and enabled architects to invoke classical (meaning Greek) precedents. Sheer height—in itself perhaps a vulgarity—began to be an aspect of form.

New York's Graham Building, designed by Clinton and Russell and finished in 1898, followed the threefold division of the Greek column: base, shaft and capital. The base was a lobby and a place for banks; the shaft a simple pattern of identical offices; and the capital, made up of attic floors, had a projecting cornice at the top. The importation of other European traditions produced, as always in Manhattan, a piquant marriage of ancient and modern. The Metropolitan Life Insurance Building, finished in 1909 by Napoleon Le Brun, was inspired by the Venetian campanile. The 60-storey Woolworth Building, which was created by Cass Gilbert in 1913 and held the record for nearly 20 years as the world's tallest building, turned European Gothic into New York Gothic.

Manhattan really got down to skyscraper business in the 1920s, the era of boom. The greatest structures—like the 77-storey Chrysler Building of William Van Alen and the 102-storey Empire State Building of Shreve, Lamb and Harmon, with its seven miles of elevator shafts and floor space for 20,000 workers—were ready by the early years of the Great Depression. Then came humbler 40-storey edifices, responding to a new spirit of sob-riety and economic caution. There also came concern about the effect of the gorgeous monsters on common civic amenity. People had to live, walk and work in the dense shadow of the man-made mountains, and life in a dark canyon can be dispiriting. In the business area, it is said, a man has to buy a newspaper to find out if the sun is shining. After the First World War a fresh kind of skyscraper sprang out of zoning laws that required the height of a building to be related to the width of the street, thus providing a statutory degree of light at street level: we may speak of the beginnings of environmental concern in New York City.

The architect Le Corbusier, who first visited New York in 1935, described it as "a beautiful and worthy catastrophe" whose architects were only just beginning to understand the problems of building a vertical city. "A skyscraper," he wrote, "should not be a coquettish plume rising up from the street. It is a wonderful instrument of concentration, to be placed in the midst of vast open spaces. The density of the skyscraper and the free area at the foot of the skyscraper constitute an indissoluble function." This new architectural thinking found its most perfect expression in the original Rockefeller Center, finished in 1940. Although it occupied a three-block site which could have accommodated the tallest monster ever seen, the designers were content with a central skyscraper of 70 storeys (the RCA building) and 13 smaller satellites. But there is more than utilitarian metal and stone. There is insistence on the value of light, air and space; and the needful is balanced by the gloriously unnecessary—landscaping, fountains, sculpture. "It is," declared Le Corbusier, "rational, logically conceived, biologically normal, harmonious in its four functional elements: halls for the entrance and division of crowds, grouped shafts for vertical circulation (elevators), corridors (internal streets), regular offices." In other words, the human and the gigantic had come to terms.

Since the Second World War, Manhattan's builders have absorbed new things from Europe. Instead of that older charming coddling of the Romanesque and Baroque and Gothic, there has been a willingness to learn from men such as Walter Gropius and Mies van der Rohe, specialists in the use of steel and glass. The so-called glass curtain wall is today the main feature of the city's graceful giants, and it represents what the aesthetic of the skyscraper is really based upon: expanse rather than simply accumulation. Pile window upon window and you have a very long, upended waffle; think in terms of a long, slim mirror and you are on the way to sorcery. The 42-storey Seagram Building, in which Mies van der Rohe joined with the American architect Philip Johnson, completing the work in 1958, is a supreme Manhattan example of what is called "the International Style".

None of this towering grandeur, however, would have been possible without the inspiration that emanated from a chance discovery. Jenney, the skyscraper pioneer, saw his wife accidentally drop a heavy book on to a frail birdcage and wondered why there was no damage. A steel frame, apparently, could absorb a considerable amount of shock. Skeletons of metal—these were the answer to the high-rise riddle. But neither Jenney nor any of the early skyscraping masters could have achieved anything without Elisha Graves Otis.

Otis was a master mechanic in a bedstead factory in Albany, New York. In 1852 his firm sent him to Yonkers, just north of New York City, there to

Towering, slab-like walls close over Pine Street in Lower Manhattan, cutting out all but a slip of sky and condemning people at ground level to perpetual twilight. But the slender elegance of a distant building reasserts that New York's vertical architecture, in spite of such gloomy side effects, deserves its renown for grandeur.

set up a new factory and to install the machinery. He was already prized as an ingenious contriver of labour-saving devices and in Yonkers he was inspired to invent an engine without which no modern megalopolis could function: the passenger elevator. Freight hoists had existed since long before his time, but the lifting rope was generally woven of hemp and apt to fray; and so the principle could not be safely adapted to passenger use. Otis introduced a safety mechanism and demonstrated it in person at the New York Exhibition in 1854. Riding into the air with the greatest of ease, he ordered that the lift rope be cut. Men gasped and women fainted, but Otis was in no danger. A clamping device gripped the guide rails of the elevator car as soon as tension was removed from the lift rope. Four years later he installed the first elevator for public use in the Haughwout Department Store. Powered by steam, it climbed five storeys in less than a minute.

By later standards, of course, this was nothing. In 1931 it took just over a minute to reach from bottom to top of the Empire State Building. Nowadays we think in terms of layered elevator banks, high-speed shuttles, sky lobbies. But the name of Otis is still in the elevator business and is rightly honoured—even if only subliminally—by many who ride the vertical air and, incuriously, see it embossed on a bulkhead. If the world of today is the world of ever higher rises, Mr Otis may be said to have launched today.

Bemused by mere extension, it is easy for us to ignore texture and colour. To enthusiasts of the humbler architecture of New York, brownstone is an inseparable part of the city's uniqueness. Once quarried on the banks of the Passaic River or in the Connecticut Valley—the oldest brownstone gravestone is that of Richard Church, buried at Trinity in 1681 at the age of five—it used to drench Manhattan like coffee. To an Englishwoman who visited the city in 1875, it seemed that every New Yorker's ambition was to live in a house with a brownstone front. "That is considered," she wrote, "the *ne plus ultra* of earthly habitations—the summit of all desires—the crowning effort of the love of make-believe. If his house looks like a nobleman's mansion in front—and you could not pay him a greater compliment than to tell him it does—the New Yorker is satisfied."

There are, in fact, many other stones in the city. White marble used to be brought by oxen to the Bronx River from the Eastchester quarries in Westchester County, and cream-coloured sandstone came from Ohio, limestone from Indiana, granite from Massachusetts. "It seems odd," wrote Henry Hope Reed, Jr. of the Museum of the City of New York, "that New York's stone has not found its poets." He had in mind not just the native varieties but also the ones imported from abroad for the glorification of the city's buildings—without and within. Stones like these:

Bleu Belge, Rose Hortensia, Botticino,
Beigenelle, Selje Cream, Bilbao Reale,
Almiscado, Tinos, Cipollino,

Appalachian Silver Grey, Meadow White Fleuri,
Vergados, Noir Blanc, Perlato Imperiale,
Rojo Toreadoro, Platina Gris.

They are all to be found there in the city, and many more besides: the steel and glass cannot have it all their own way.

The German film director Fritz Lang, seeing the Manhattan skyline from a ship, was impelled to start thinking of a film project about the city of the future. His film, *Metropolis*, appeared in 1926 and its cut-out, studio-made skyscrapers mingled, in the dreams of this Manchester schoolboy, with the true enfilmed and photographed Manhattan. It helped to make New York seem sinister as well as magical. *Metropolis* not only tells the story of urban machine-slaves buried deep in hovels beneath the concrete giants; it recapitulates the myth of the Tower of Babel. "Let us build a tower that will reach the sky": God was not pleased, and in his anger he confounded the language of the builders.

The myth has, to some extent, been enacted in New York, although with no dire consequences as yet. The city is the official home of all the nations, and all the languages of the world jostle together happily enough. If there is a curse lying on New York, it has nothing to do with language. One expects a curse to be imposed on a place that so seems to defy Nature, or God, or ordinary human possibility; and one finds it implied in certain questions. Is a city of nearly eight million people really governable? Can it bear the load—its traditional pride—of looking after the poor and shiftless and alienated? Can it consume and pollute without retribution from Nature (or God)? The generalized sense of fear or foreboding or *hubris* has always been there, felt most intensely by the New Yorkers themselves, in whom the city's deeper character is to be found. It is time for me to stop looking at the skyline and start looking at the people.

Manhattan Kingdom

PHOTOGRAPHS BY DAN BUDNIK

JAY MAISEL

With the Empire State Building aflame in the glow of the setting sun, the skyscrapers of Manhattan's midtown business district rear up behind the Hudson River.

New York's centrepiece, the borough of Manhattan, is a city in its own right—and like none other on earth. The giant buildings that parade its 22 square miles make it an island fortress of enterprise and commerce; its resident population —a scant 1.5 million—is more than doubled each day by workers from the four outlying boroughs of New York and by armies of commuters from the suburbs. Securely rooted in solid rock—scraped clean 20,000 years ago by Ice Age glaciers —its skyscrapers tower into fairyland crenellations, as if crowded skywards by the encompassing moat of rivers. As seen from across the surrounding waters and from the air in these six classic Manhattan views, the island's exotic battlements take on a majestic unity that is accentuated by the weather; and glass by the mile mirrors the moods of sky and water.

The twin towers of the World Trade Center, each a quarter of a mile high and housing 22,000 workers, guard the north-western flanks of Manhattan's financial district: Wall Street. Around them as seen from the abandoned piers of New Jersey, traditional and modern skyscrapers crowd together above the narrow streets of what was once the 17th-Century Dutch outpost of New Amsterdam.

Manhattan's notched skyline, dominated by the Empire State Building, looms eerily through fog and fumes hanging at sunset over suburban homes. The perspective is from Throgs Neck in the Bronx, ten miles away to the north-east.

An aerial view from across the East River, with the Queensboro Bridge in the foreground, emphasizes Manhattan's thronged narrowness. From the United Nations Building (right), it is a mere two miles across the city to the banks of the Hudson River on which stand the dominating towers of the World Trade Center.

Thrown like a drawbridge from upper Manhattan (left) to the New Jersey cliffs, the George Washington Bridge is the island's only above-ground link across the Hudson—choked here with ice. Built in 1931 and slung with 105,000 miles of cable, the bridge was strong enough to support a second roadway, successfully added beneath the first in 1962.

Manhattan at dusk is transformed by light and snow into a jewel-box city. The two glittering square miles framed here encompass, it has been said, the busiest, most energy-consuming, highest-earning urban area on earth.

2

An Array of Influences

The story of New York is a story of immigrant battling with immigrant, ceasing to battle with immigrant, but always ready to battle with new immigrant. No place in the world has been so rich in the diversity of its new arrivals. A century ago, when New York City (then still synonymous with Manhattan) had a population of about a million, nearly half had been born overseas. As long ago as the 1640s, 18 languages were being spoken amongst the island's few hundred settlers. That was at a time when men and women came in a desperation that could be measured in the rigours of an ocean voyage that took up to 24 weeks, in conditions so wretched that one-third of their number could be expected to die before even reaching Manhattan's shores.

Two centuries later the wretchedness of the immigrants had hardly abated, had even intensified, and the voyage—at least for the steerage passengers—was still damnable enough. On fast, light packets purpose-built at Bremen in Germany for immigrant traffic, the journey now took about 14 weeks, and while first-class passengers ate well and drank champagne the steerage occupants slept in the gangways, swabbed down decks and worked in the galleys, living in an enforced stink of poverty and vomit.

Ancestral voyages continue to form part of the mythology of New York, contributing to legends of hell in Europe and purgatory on the high seas —all of them rooted in terrible truth. When one of the ships arrived after 96 days from Hamburg, the below-decks passengers had been without drinking water for 42 of them. Cholera was rife and a third of the intending immigrants were too ill to leave their bunks when the ship reached New York. If the German ships were bad, the French and English ships were worse—the most appalling of all being those that carried the Irish. A Quebec newspaper said, in 1847, that "the Black Hole of Calcutta was a mercy compared to the holds of these vessels". Although the coming of steam in the second half of the 19th Century shortened the voyages to a couple of weeks, they were still nasty and brutal.

Why did they come? Because of worklessness, hunger, political oppression, racial and religious persecution. Why did they stay in New York? Often for no more reason than that it was the end of the voyage: after such journeys, no wonder that, as at last they kissed the New York earth, many had no desire to travel farther. Here was America enough: why continue the journey west, east or south? Moreover, if nostalgia became too strong, this was the nearest American port to Europe—still hell but also the old home. Besides, after the Erie Canal was opened in 1825, linking New York to the Great Lakes, the city became a mecca of westward expansion, a place where a man could always be sure of earning a decent wage—and might even end up making a fortune.

Unscrupulous shipping agents in Europe, ever anxious to secure the largest possible share of the lucrative trade in emigrants, touted the attractions of New York. Typical were the blandishments offered by one firm in 1837. Prospective clients in Britain were assured that "everyone was on a perfect equality in America; that the common labouring man received high wages and sat at the same table with his master . . . and that with ease an independent fortune could be made".

The first great wave of immigrants began to break on New York's shores in the 1840s and was composed largely of Irish fleeing the potato famine that was then devastating their homeland. These Celtic Catholics encountered Nordic Protestants already in possession, and New York's ethnic problems had begun. That primal situation, although supposedly resolved, has left a ghost of peculiar potency: the popular notion of a ruling class of White Anglo-Saxon Protestants or WASPs.

The WASP myth is not strictly accurate, just as the term itself is tautologous (an Anglo-Saxon is necessarily white). We may take it that in, say, 1656 the thousand inhabitants of Manhattan comprised German, Scandinavian, English and Scottish settlers as well as the original Dutch. Call them Teutonic Protestants or Teutprots rather than WASPs. They made up a kind of Manhattan master race and, in spite of much dilution since then, the American physical prototype—in film, sport or international beauty contest—tends, in the world's eyes, still to be tall, blond, Teutprot.

In just 15 years the population of Manhattan more than doubled, swelling from 371,000 in 1845 to 813,000 in 1860, and the new New Yorkers included many Germans as well as Irishmen. Isabella Bird, the daughter of an English missionary, visited New York in 1854 and watched the immigrants streaming off the ships.

"The goods and chattels of the Irish," she wrote later, "appeared to consist principally of numerous red-haired, unruly children, and ragged-looking bundles tied round with rope. The Germans were generally ruddy and stout, and took as much care of their substantial-looking, well-corded, heavy chests as though they contained gold. The English appeared pale and debilitated, and sat helpless and weary-looking on their boxes."

It was not only in their appearance and possessions that the Irish and German immigrants differed. The Irish, although English-speaking and legal children of Great Britain, were looked down upon because they were Catholic, while the Germans, knowing no English, were acceptable because they were Protestant. Protestantism was the religion of hard work, cleanliness, education, advancement. The faith of Dante and Michelangelo was associated with shiftlessness, squalor, indolence and ignorance.

An immigrant boy, newly arrived in Manhattan from Ellis Island's immigration station, submits to a city Health Officer probing for symptoms of fever during the typhus scare of 1911. Two other youngsters await their turn beneath a scrawled sign that most of the newcomers would have been unable to read.

Although the Germans had an easier time than the Irish, yet power and position (if not necessarily cultural prestige) passed eventually to the greater number, and the Irish were soon by far the most powerful single nationality group in the city. "Irishmen to your post, or you'll lose America," declaimed an election poster of the period. "By perseverance you may become its rulers. By negligence you will become its slaves. Your own country was lost by submitting to ambitious rulers. This beautiful country you can gain by being firm and united. Vote the tickets Alexander Stewart, Alderman; Edward Flannagan, Assessor; both true Irishmen."

By the 1870s, when Manhattan's population was approaching a million, more than one-fifth had been born in Ireland, and the Teutprot element, now strongly Germanic, was on the defensive. There were two consequences, both familiar enough to present-day New Yorkers. The first was simple racial strife. The Irish and the Germans hated each other, and both groups fought their battles in and out of the taverns and spilled blood on the streets. The second was a middle-class drift to the suburbs—what are now the boroughs of Brooklyn, Queens, the Bronx and Staten Island —where the orderly, tranquil Teutprots hoped to escape contamination by the dirty, turbulent Irish of Manhattan.

By now another problem, also depressingly familiar to present-day New Yorkers, had manifested itself: the conflict of black and white. I had better say now that I use the term "black" under duress. The blackest people I know are the Tamils of Madras and Jaffna, and they call themselves not blacks but Indians. "Black", as used in America, has a very parochial ring and the expression assumes a cultural, racial and political unity hardly subscribed to by all the blacks outside America. "Afro-American" would be a more accurate term, but "black" has been sanctified by black insistence on its use. Of this I say no more.

Slavery had flourished in New York under both the British and the Americans, but after the Revolution increasing numbers of blacks succeeded in buying their freedom and in 1827 total emancipation was proclaimed in the State of New York. But discrimination against blacks persisted and New York was one of the few Northern cities to return fugitive slaves to the South. "Are there laws against Negroes?" asked an incredulous French visitor to the city. "Are they outside the common law? No: but public prejudice persecutes them more tyranically than any law. They are denied the omnibuses, are excluded from the churches. That's how these democrats interpret equality, and these Puritans, Christian charity."

It is perhaps not surprising that many of the newly arrived Irish immigrants, who were themselves despised and rejected by the haughty Teutprot Establishment, used the blacks as convenient scapegoats for their frustration and resentment. Barred from the professions and most of the trades, blacks also competed with the Irish for jobs. While work was plentiful, the antagonism of the immigrants was more or less controlled. But in

1857 a financial panic hit the city and, with one-seventh of the population on relief and angry demonstrations of unemployed marching through the streets, some observers feared the worst. "The financial crisis," noted one New Yorker in his diary, "has thrown thousands of the working class out of employment and made it difficult matter enough to maintain peace and order in the city through the winter."

The day of reckoning, however, had not yet arrived; and a crisis of rather more heroic proportions was soon engaging the city's attention. In April, 1861, the American Civil War began and within three weeks New Yorkers had subscribed more than $2 million to the Union cause. According to the correspondent of *The Times* of London, the city's merchants had been reluctant to offend their Southern friends; but convinced finally of the South's determination to quit the Union, "they resolved to avert the permanent loss of the great profits derived from their connection with the South by some present sacrifices. They rushed to the platforms—the battlecry was sounded from almost every pulpit—flag raising took place in every square . . . and the oath was taken to trample Secession under foot, and to quench the fire of the Southern heart forever".

But pro-Southern sentiment was by no means extinguished in New York and as the war dragged on enthusiasm for the Union diminished. In March, 1863, Lincoln issued a call for 300,000 men and it was announced that conscription would begin in New York on Saturday, July 11. The new Conscription Law not only authorized the enlistment of blacks, but also enabled rich whites to buy their way out of military service for $300— two provisions that naturally enraged New York's immigrant workforce.

On July 13 the city erupted. Mobs of mainly Irish labourers rampaged through the streets, looting, burning and killing. Blacks were their special targets and scores were beaten, tortured and killed. Many were burned alive or hanged from trees and lamp-posts, and the Coloured Orphan Asylum on Fifth Avenue was burned down. Warships trained their guns on the city and after five days of bloody clashes, during which troops used artillery against the mob, the rioting ended. While the North was still reckoning the cost of its victory over the Confederate forces of General Lee at Gettysburg earlier that same July, New York counted its own casualties: more than ten thousand, including at least two thousand killed.

For more than a decade after the end of the Civil War the Irish continued to make up the bulk of new immigrants.

In the 1880s, however, a new inrush of immigrants began. This time the newcomers were Southern Italians and Jews from Eastern Europe, and the double thrust continued until new federal laws of the 1920s cut down very sharply on the numbers permitted to enter. The huge Italian waves, subsiding as rock-pools in Mulberry Street and Bleecker Street, or in East Harlem and Staten Island, came mostly from Sicily and Naples. Using a Spanish loan-word, the Neapolitans call themselves *guapi*, meaning "pretty

The large electric flame atop the Statue of Liberty's 29-foot-long torch glows brightly in the early dusk.

Freedom's Beacon

Raising her torch aloft, the colossal Statue of Liberty—originally titled "Liberty Enlightening the World"—stands elegantly planted on a concrete pedestal at the entrance to New York City's harbour. Presented as a gift from France to celebrate the centenary of America's independence and unveiled in 1886, the 151-foot-tall copper statue was designed by the Alsatian sculptor Frédéric Bartholdi and represents Liberty breaking free of the shackles of tyranny. Its wrought-iron interior framework was designed by Gustave Eiffel, who later built Paris's Eiffel Tower. Once a lodestar to hopeful immigrants, it is still regarded as a symbol of American democracy.

Viewed straight on from a helicopter the Statue of Liberty seems taller and thinner than when viewed from below. In her left arm she carries a tablet that commemorates the Declaration of Independence with the date July 4, 1776, in raised roman numerals. The right arm is 42 feet long and 12 feet in diameter; the forefinger is eight feet long.

An observation eyrie inside the crown is reached by elevator and a final 168 spiralled steps. In the wavy lines of the domed area are the impressions of Liberty's tresses. The statue's skin, covering Eiffel's framework, consists of more than 300 sheets of copper, each 3/32 inch thick, hammered together and weighing a total of 90 tons.

From a giddy, aerial perspective obtained by few visitors, the broken shackles symbolic of tyranny can be seen jutting out from beneath the figure's robe.

ones", and here we have the origin of the derisive "wop". The North—Turin, Milan, Genoa, Bologna, Florence—has never been greatly represented in Manhattan's Little Italy, and the ignorant may be tempted to make false generalizations about Italian *mores* and culture from the evidence of the translated South.

The New York Italian cuisine, for instance, is notable for pasta, tomato sauce, pizza—all of which are very southern. Every American knows what a pizza is, but not every Milanese is familiar with it. In Bologna there is no great interest in spaghetti, and Florence—like Kansas City—specializes in extremely large beefsteaks. The massive devotion to San Gennaro in Manhattan's Little Italy, which devotes a festival to him in late September each year, results from his being the patron saint of Naples. The less wholesome importation of the Mafia has, in origin, nothing to do with mainland Italy, only with Sicily. Northern Italians say that Italy is Europe and Sicily is Africa. The distinction is grotesque, but it is a reminder that all that is Sicilian is not necessarily characteristic of the rest of Italy.

The arrival of the Southern Italians confirmed Teutprots in their belief that Catholicism was the faith of squalor and shiftlessness. Even the Italian dramatist, Guiseppe Giacosa, who came to New York in 1891 to direct Sarah Bernhardt in a performance of his *La Dame de Challant*, was appalled by the living conditions of his compatriots.

"Men in tattered, filthy attire move from one shop to another," he wrote later, "or form small groups at the entrances of those beer taverns where they are served the bitter dregs of the barrels from which beer is sold in healthy quarters to healthy people. In the doorways, on the steps of the staircases, on little wooden and straw stools almost in the middle of the street, women carry on all the pursuits of their pathetic domestic life. They nurse their young, sew, clean the withered greens which are the only ingredient of their soup, wash their clothes in grimy tubs, untangle and arrange one another's hair. They chatter, not in the happy mood of Naples, but in a certain angry importuning way that stings the heart."

Like the Irish, the Southern Italians were forced by poverty into low-rent areas where squalor was already entrenched. But neither group was lazy. The vast amount of construction that turned New York into the world's greatest port and entrepreneur was in the hands of these Catholic labourers, who fed on starch but had fine muscles and incredible endurance.

Not that the two major Catholic peoples of the city were inclined to make their religion a bond. Father Flanagan or Father O'Brien was ready to welcome the newcomers into his church, but there was the divisive question of language and culture. The Italians built their own churches and did not feel compelled to confess their sins in English. And, very notably, the Italians remained one of the immigrant groups too satisfied with their own culture to wish to modify it through the contagion of inter-marriage. Even now the family is strong and priests are respected. The Italians have

From New Amsterdam to New York

1524	Italian navigator Giovanni da Verrazano discovers bay where New York City now stands
1609	British Captain Henry Hudson, in employ of Dutch East India Company, sails up the river later named for him, in search of inland passage to Orient; reaches present-day Albany
1614	Dutch explore Long Island Sound area and lay claim to it as New Netherland
1626	Peter Minuit, director-general of Dutch colony, purchases "Manhates Island" from Indians for 60 guilders worth of goods. Names colony of 200 Dutch and Walloon settlers at tip of island "New Amsterdam"
1639	Jonas Bronck buys parcel of land from Indians, later to become the Bronx
1646	First cargo of Negroes to be sold as slaves arrives in New Amsterdam from Brazil
1647	Peter Stuyvesant arrives to become director-general of New Amsterdam
1653	City population reaches 800. Municipal government set up; City Tavern converted to City Hall
1658	Village of Harlem founded
1664	British fleet, sent by Duke of York during English–Dutch War, captures New Amsterdam. Duke renames city "New York"
1698	Completion of Trinity Church at Wall Street. Among donators of funds is Captain William Kidd, the pirate
1703	Battery of cannon installed at southern tip of Manhattan (hence name "The Battery")
1725	City's first newspaper, The New-York Gazette, appears
1754	King's College—now Columbia University—established
1762	Samuel Fraunces, a Negro, opens Fraunces Tavern, still standing at Pearl and Broad Streets
1763	City population reaches 12,000
1765	Stamp Act Congress, including delegates from nine colonies, protests against tax imposed by Parliament on such items as legal documents, pamphlets, newspapers and dice
1776	War of Independence begins. British land at Kips Bay and capture New York. Fire levels one-third of city, including Trinity Church
1783	Upon signing of final peace treaty in Paris, British evacuate New York. General George Washington holds victory dinner in Fraunces Tavern
1785	New York becomes temporary capital of new nation
1789	First Congress under the Constitution meets at City Hall, now called Federal Hall. George Washington is inaugurated as President on balcony
1800	City's population reaches 60,000
1803	Yellow fever epidemic hits city, resulting in suspension of business and some 600 deaths
1807	Robert Fulton sails world's first steamship, the "Clermont" on East River
1812	First Tammany Hall, home of city's Democratic Party, completed
1816	Brooklyn incorporated as village
1820	New York becomes nation's most populated city with more than 120,000 inhabitants
1833	First house built for tenant families—a "tenement house"—on Water Street
1835	"Great Fire" destroys almost 700 buildings in centre of city
1837	Population of city approaches 300,000. One-sixth of island occupied by houses, business establishments; remainder is gardens and farms. Financial panic; all but three banks close their doors

1840	Construction begins on new Trinity Church at Wall Street
1845	Second "Great Fire" rages. More than 300 buildings demolished and 30 lives taken. Knickerbocker Baseball Club of New York is founded; nation's first formally organized team for game that became "national pastime"
1853	First World's Fair in U.S. held in Crystal Palace—exact replica of London's Crystal Palace—on present site of New York Public Library and Bryant Park
1863	Civil War riots erupt; more than a thousand lives lost
1876	Official opening of Central Park, designed by Frederick Law Olmsted and Calvert Vaux
1878	Sixth Avenue and Third Avenue Els (elevated railroads) inaugurated
1879	St. Patrick's Cathedral, under construction since 1858, completed
1880	Manhattan population reaches one million. After ten years of temporary housing, Metropolitan Museum of Art is moved permanently to Central Park
1883	Brooklyn Bridge, first span over East River, is completed
1886	Dedication of "Liberty Enlightening the World" (Statue of Liberty), commemorating centenary of Declaration of Independence
1892	Ellis Island replaces Castle Garden as immigration station
1896	Thomas A. Edison's vitascope projects first motion-pictures exhibition at the Koster & Bial Music Hall
1898	Five boroughs of Manhattan, Brooklyn, Queens, Staten Island and Bronx are united to form Greater New York, an area of 359 square miles with total population of three million
1902	Completion of Flatiron Building at 23rd Street and Fifth Avenue
1903	Williamsburg Bridge, world's longest suspension design, opens. Marconi's wireless telegraph established between New York and England
1904	First subway line operates from City Hall to West 145th Street
1909	Completion of Manhattan and Queensboro Bridges
1910	Pennsylvania Railroad Station begins service
1911	New York Public Library opens at 42nd Street and 5th Avenue
1913	Completion of 792-foot-high Woolworth Building, then world's tallest. Grand Central Station opens
1927	Holland Tunnel, under Hudson River between Manhattan and New Jersey, completed
1929	Wall Street Crash. Panic selling of millions of shares on New York Stock Exchange marks beginning of world economic crisis
1931	Completion of Empire State Building and George Washington Bridge
1936	Triborough Bridge—connecting Manhattan, Bronx and Queens—completed
1939	World's Fair begins at Flushing Meadows in Queens
1946	City selected as headquarters for United Nations
1948	International Airport at Idlewild in Queens begins operations
1952	United Nations Security Council and General Assembly inaugurate buildings at permanent site on banks of East River
1964	New York World's Fair launched
1965	Pope Paul visits New York to plead for peace at United Nations. Electric power failure darkens entire city
1973	Completion of 110-storey twin-tower World Trade Center
1975	City verges on default of obligations. Municipal Assistance Corporation ("Big Mac") set up by state to reorganize city's finances

not proselytized on behalf of Dante and Ariosto. They keep to themselves, and their monuments are culinary.

The Jewish population of New York represents less an influx of refugees from European poverty (although that came into it) than a flight from pro-longed Slav and Teutonic persecution. More Jews live here than in any other city of the world: some two million, a quarter of the entire Greater New York population and more than four times as many as inhabit Israel's largest metropolis, the twin cities of Tel Aviv–Jaffa. Their cultural influence, from colloquial speech and cuisine to music and literature, now thoroughly saturates this city that once regarded them as pariahs.

The Jews served to unite Protestants and Catholics in a common fear and dislike of the children of Israel. The Irish and Italians might be alien and Catholic, but at least they were Christian. The Jews, however, were almost outlandishly alien as well as blatantly non-Christian, forming what Theodore Dreiser called the city's "most radical foreign plexus". They were also industrious and thoughtful, and had powerful preoccupations with hygiene, which did them no good at all, except perhaps spiritually.

A pattern in New York's demographic history should now be visible. Each fresh influx of immigrants is despised and feared, and detestable qualities are attributed to its members. As the new settlers settle, the old inhabitants want to get out. They abdicate power, and a new "establishment" to fill the yawning vacuum is created out of old riff-raff. When we hear the same perennial foul attributions applied to the newest immigrants—the postwar blacks and Puerto Ricans—we do not have to take them totally seriously. It is true that the new settlers, like many of their predecessors, have to live in slums among small-time criminals, and that their consequent fights to survive often take an anti-social form. But what looks like congenital criminality now may one day be viewed in retrospect as justifiable aggression by people shouldering to find a place in the sun.

Before considering the blacks and Puerto Ricans in more detail, I will deal with one group of immigrants to New York who are not definable by race, language or religion. Nor does their arrival in the city slip neatly into a chronological slot; they have been coming here virtually since it was founded, although most notably during the first half of this century (many of them lured, no doubt, by those same movies I saw in Manchester). They do not share a single culture and have not staked out one particular neighbourhood as their own. Their numbers are difficult to extract from census tables, but there have been many of them, and their impact, although unmeasured, is certainly profound.

They are Americans who have come here from other parts of the United States in order to try their teeth on "The Big Apple", as they call New York, implying disdain for those who seek their fortune in other and less dazzling American cities. They may be Catholics, Protestants, Jews, Zen Buddhists,

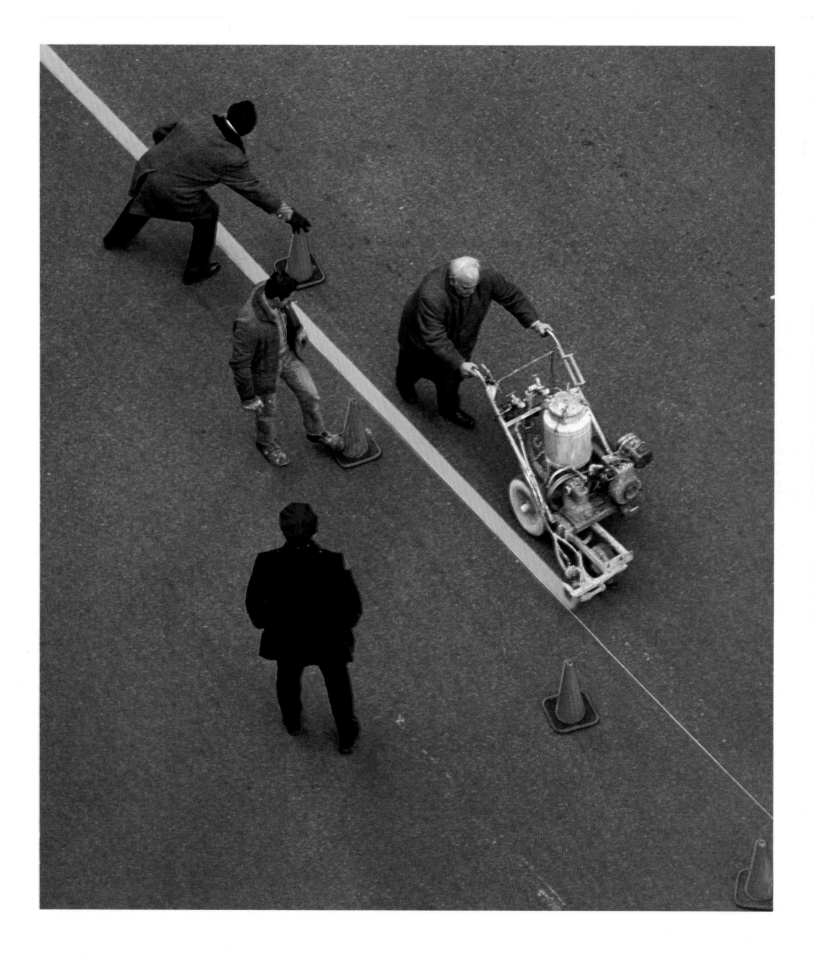

With Irish blood strong among its citizens, New York makes St. Patrick's Day—March 17—one of its biggest annual celebrations. The white line on the parade's route up Fifth Avenue is painted green the day before (left), and participants in the parade itself find endless variations on the emerald theme—such as green carnations, green bowlers or even a white horse tinted green (above).

or agnostics, but for most of these immigrants from America the only serious religion is ambition. Some are from poor homes, some from wealthy ones; all hope to be richer for coming to New York.

Not for them the foreign immigrant tradition of starting at the very bottom of the heap. They have tended to enter New York laterally, sidling in somewhere above the poverty level, and the closest they have come to the Ellis Island experience is arriving at the bus station, leather suitcases in their hands, names of friends of friends to look up in their pockets and in their minds dreams of "making it" as artist/super salesman/writer/dancer/ advertising executive/musician/lawyer/stockbroker. They head not for the slums but for the YMCA or YWCA. Or, if their entry is cushioned by a giant corporation that hired them in Detroit or Houston and now feels they are ready for the big-time world of the head office, they come by air to Kennedy or La Guardia and take a cab to a midtown hotel.

Arriving singly rather than as part of a recognizable mass-migration, they meet little of the resentment that has been directed at more obvious newcomers, although their everyday encounters with policemen, taxi-drivers and muggers initially may make them feel otherwise. Depending on how they fare, they may stay a couple of weeks or the rest of their lives. Some, defeated or disgusted or homesick, go back to Des Moines. A hand-ful—who is to say whether they won or lost?—end up as street freaks haunting Times Square or the drop-out neighbourhoods.

Most achieve moderate success, marry and move to the suburbs, becoming part-time New Yorkers—if that is the correct term for the species that inhabits Manhattan's skyscrapers between 9 a.m. and 6 p.m. on week-days. (In some of those awesome towers you rarely meet a person born in New York City, and almost never one born in Manhattan.) The few who truly make it big can afford to stay in the city even after dark and are to be found in expensive apartments on the East Side, preferably overlooking Central Park or the East River from a high altitude.

Being Americans before they arrived, and mainly white, sober and industrious Americans at that, these immigrants have not noticeably disturbed the city's ethnological mixture, which was given a chance to settle after the strict controls of the 1920s curbed immigration from abroad. It is striking that New York's three decades of relative racial peace belong to the interregnum that began then and ended in the 1950s and 1960s, when the great influx of blacks and Puerto Ricans started. The arrival of these newest New Yorkers started demographic shifts more dramatic than any known in previous phases of the city's history. More than a million whites of European origin left New York while a million Puerto Ricans and blacks from the southern states came to the city. Blacks and Puerto Ricans together, in the the mid-1970s, numbered two and a half million.

The inability of New York to close the black–white division is the most disturbing feature of recent years. That division has remained static at a time when desegregation has been the watchword of the American courts, if not of all the American people. There have been signs that segregation, following some subterranean law, intensified in direct proportion to the law's insistence on desegregation. New York City's 2,159 census districts show very clearly the unhealthy imbalance of black–white distribution. As of 1970 more than two-thirds of these districts were either almost wholly black or wholly white. Equally alarmingly, 80 per cent of the black population lived in what were officially designated as poverty areas.

The black world is alien to all but a very few whites. I have entered it only through literature. To know the black experience, as I did, read Ralph Ellison's *Invisible Man*. This novel, first published in 1952, tells us more about the black–white problem in New York, and elsewhere, than a whole library of cold documents. The black narrator calls himself invisible because "people refuse to see me . . . . When they approach me they see only my surroundings, themselves, or figments of their imagination—indeed, everything and anything except me". The book was in my mind one day when I walked through Harlem, the only white man around, and met neither hostility nor curiosity but a kind of willed indifference. I became myself an invisible man. I escaped as quickly as I could back to my white world.

But there is no escape for Ellison's nameless hero. He is condemned to working in a paint factory that has the slogan: "Keep America Pure with Liberty Paints." His task is to produce a white paint by dropping some magical substance into black liquid. This liquid, stirred by a black finger, is essential for the making of pure whiteness: the black keeps America pure by becoming a scapegoat for its sins. There are apocalyptical visions of wholesale destruction, sacrifice, the end of the world; there is a dream of escape to a symbolic black hole where the black is truly invisible—although, like a coal mine, that hole is the eventual source of heat and light.

The book does not end with the orthodox plea for integration or black conquest that we may expect. Instead, it says: "Why, if they follow this conformity business they'll end up by forcing me, an invisible man, to become white, which is not a colour but a lack of one." We need what New York potentially has: the glory of diversity. When we can all see this, there will be no need for talk of toleration, or of revenge, conquest and destruction.

At the moment, however, the problems of diversity overwhelm any sense of glory. It has been pointed out repeatedly that the black–white confrontation in New York can find no parallel in the various racial and religious enmities of the 19th Century. Immigrant Irish, Germans, Italians, Jews, Poles were animated by no racial ideologies: they desired to go their own way as far as they could, but not so far as to militate against the basic New York philosophy. This wisdom, as old as the original Anglo–Dutch settlement, in effect says: For God's sake let's live and let live, and try to earn a living. The post-war blacks recognize that their dissatisfactions and animosities are not only parochial but also universal. There is an international

From his tenement window a young Puerto Rican boy keeps a quiet, proprietorial eye over treasured possessions: bicycle parts too big to store within a small, crowded apartment. Since 1910 the Puerto Rican population has increased from 500 to over a million, many of whom occupy similarly cramped quarters.

racist philosophy around and a frequently garbled concept of pan-Africanism that sees all blacks—but not all men—as brothers.

The settling down of blacks, and white Puerto Ricans as well, into just plain New Yorkers is going to take a very long time. It is true that, in certain very important respects, these latest newcomers are not so badly off as many of the earlier immigrants. Even in the first years of this century men and women froze to death on the streets or in dank cellars, died of tuberculosis (the "Jewish disease"), were thrown out of their miserable tenements after a month's failure to pay the rent. There was no welfare then as there is now. Moreover, no racial animosities, however demented, reach the bizarre limits of the old xenophobia.

Bureaucratic immigration officers on Ellis Island even insisted on garbling immigrant names into something Teutprottishly acceptable. Novelist Irving Wallace is so named because an immigration officer found his father's "Wallechinsky" too difficult to record. Foreign tongues were a joke and foreign accents an index of stupidity. Nowadays immigrant languages are being taken seriously, as well as ethnic *moeurs*. One day I heard an Irish policeman speaking very earnestly to a Puerto Rican corner-boy in Spanish, even using subjunctives.

All this is encouraging, but does not alter the fact that the present situation is explosive. The blacks and Puerto Ricans are young, and youth tends to violence either out of the need to deploy spare energy, or else out of social frustrations that old age sadly learns to live with. Statistics show that New York's blacks are on average more than ten years younger than

New York's European whites, and the city's Puerto Ricans are younger still. The violence, then, of these two groups is not to be explained by some unique racial inheritance of original sin. The youth of all the major cities of the world tends, and has always tended, to violence, but New York is a special case. No city anywhere at any time has known such pressures of adjustment consequent on rapid population growth, with the population itself so bizarrely multiracial and polyglot.

To understand the problem, however, is not to solve it. Violence always has to be dealt with. Sociologists—translating the term into some such shibboleth as "anti-social behaviour" and thus assigning to themselves responsibility for solving the problem—say that education is the only answer. If that is true, the prospect is gloomy so far as Puerto Rican and black youth are concerned. For their very numbers ensure that they flood the public schools, while their backgrounds guarantee great difficulty in maintaining the same standards as the non-Puerto Rican whites. It is not, of course, a question of intelligence but of poverty and of familial conservatism. One cannot step out of a bookless home provided by Spanish-speaking parents into a school with a curriculum dedicated to the conservation of Anglo-Saxon culture and hope to get far.

Tests taken by more than half a million pupils in Queens and Brooklyn have shown a steady decline in reading ability as compared with the rest of the United States. The more impoverished the area, the greater the backwardness—often two or even three years behind the national average. In middle-income districts, on the other hand, pupils were sometimes two years ahead of it. I do not believe that children from these more fortunate areas are necessarily less anti-social than their poorer and less literate counterparts. But I do believe that decent living conditions can be fine solvents of anti-social behaviour.

As long ago as 1890, Jacob Riis, a crusader on behalf of New York's under-privileged and himself an immigrant from Denmark, wrote: "A map of the city, coloured to designate nationalities, would show more stripes than on the skin of a zebra, and more colours than any rainbow." Today's ethnic map is hardly less varied and territorial boundaries are still rigidly defined. The blacks have their impenetrable strongholds of Harlem and Brooklyn's Bedford-Stuyvesant. The Puerto Ricans established their first beachhead in East Harlem, moved west into *West Side Story* territory and later crossed the bridge to Brooklyn, even—some of the more fortunate ones—climbing to the choice neighbourhood of Brooklyn Heights.

The Chinese are in Chinatown in southern Manhattan and the Hungarians are between 70th and 79th Streets on Second Avenue. The Scandinavians favour Bay Ridge in Brooklyn. The Poles leave 7th and 8th Streets on the first Sunday in October to parade their national culture and non-Irish Catholicism down Fifth Avenue. The Irish are dispersed through

Taking full advantage of the mid-morning late winter sun, bundled-up chess-players confront each other over their boards in Washington Square Park. Popular among early European immigrants, the game retains a wide appeal. In Manhattan's parks alone, the city's Parks Department has built 380 concrete chess tables for young and old alike.

all the boroughs, and they take over Manhattan vigorously on March 17—St. Patrick's Day.

Their devotion to the national saint far outdoes anything to be seen in the mother country, and—for a single day, at least—it infects the non-Irish, even the non-Christian, New Yorker. Booked once to give a talk on existentialism to a studious Manhattan group that was almost wholly Jewish, I was reminded by my audience that it was March 17 and that I had better talk on James Joyce instead. After the talk we all got drunk and sang *Come Back to Erin* and *When Irish Eyes Are Smiling* (most of the best Irish ballads were composed in New York, some of them by Jews). Macy's department store had, one St. Patrick's Day, the advertisements, *Bagels begorrah —Green Yet!* At such a time one sees what New York is meant to be all about.

Today's religious toleration is interpreted by the cynical as mere indifferentism; but were it simply indifferent to religion New York probably would not manage to maintain nearly four thousand places of worship. The Catholics and the Jews have made the city seem, in terms of faith, a bizarre theological Byzantium where religious issues untouched by reformation can be aired without embarrassment. Terms like *evil* ring hollow in London, but the city's Press has invoked fundamental theological phraseology in discussing the My-Lai Massacre or New York's daily violence.

Such diversity creates a desperate problem for an author striving to convert this mass of immigrant souls into flesh and blood. I can talk of New Yorkers but it is much more difficult to show what a New Yorker is like.

Under a clutter of signs and cheap clothes, Sunday afternoon bargain-hunters saunter through the market stalls of Orchard Street on the Lower East Side.

It would be too easy to parade cartoon stereotypes: the Irish cop, the Italian restaurateur, the reactionary construction worker (or "hard hat", as he is called here).

I get some help from novels. The frightening and exhausting urban experience has been so well set down by New York writers that life in this city has become a world paradigm for all city life. They have produced books like Ellison's *Invisible Man* and Henry Roth's *Call It Sleep*, which shows with unforgettable power the initiation of a sensitive Jewish child into New York's slum-world, where a people with proud traditions and a noble language are degraded into gutter-crawling mouthers of deformed quasi-English. On the other hand, all such "ethnic" literature is divisive. The glory of diversity must presuppose a unity. We are still a long way—in life as in literature, its mirror—from the image of a New Yorker *per se*: one who is defined by his city as much as by his supra-racial humanity.

Nevertheless, I am about to attempt a generalization, and I know it is going to be false, like all generalizations. But without generalization one cannot communicate at all. In general, then, the New Yorker seems to me self-concerned to a degree not found in London. His philosophy, his religion, is himself; but it is a self of a somewhat superficial kind: flashy, presented with swift brush-strokes to the observer or interlocutor, designed to impress through a kind of wit, a pithiness of speech, a wide but shallow knowledge of ephemera, smartness, a surface elegance. To him (as James Joyce put it) sufficient unto the day is the newspaper thereof—although even the newspaper is scanned rapidly and superficially. When the evening comes, even the morning is old stuff; and yesterday is ancient history. The cult of the new is as close to a unifying philosophy as New York, and especially Manhattan, can reach.

The New Yorker is equipped with the lineaments of the super salesman. His personality is devised to appear in full light, without shadows, and mirrors the figuration of Manhattan. Straight, thin lines shoot up into the air along desperately straight streets and avenues. Nothing—save in the old downtown area, which expresses the convoluted European conscious-ness—must look like a thoroughfare drawn freehand. There is a certain alarming charm in the attempt of a city to lay itself out "rationally", making arithmetic as well as Euclidian geometry out of its street-plan, and even taking a certain pride in refusing to accept the renaming of Sixth Avenue as the Avenue of the Americas. What is an undoubted convenience—you cannot easily lose your way in most parts of Manhattan, unless you are a drug-taking gypsy cab-driver—is also inhuman. The inhumanity does not quite work: the streets and numbered avenues find their way into songs and become as flavoursome as London's Old Kent Road and Paris's Boul' Mich'—but the stamp of rationality remains.

The kind of New Yorker I have, with New York superficiality, tried to delineate is made for—or is made by—this angled city, where there are no

Dickensian alleys and courts and sly taverns and lawyers' chambers at the top of twisting, worm-eaten stairs. It is a city of the straight-line, go-getting, conscious mind, which does not observe the steam of hell that comes swirling out of the street gratings.

Obsessed with himself, the New Yorker hardly sees his city. If he looked closely at it, he would be shocked at the squalor he has made there. New York is perhaps the dirtiest major city in the Western world. The street-cleaners cannot keep pace with the dog faeces, the crushed cans and the masses of waste paper. Sometimes, to the visitor, the don't-give-a-damn attitude to the environment can be summed up in a triviality, such as the crammed ashtray of the reception desk in a Park Avenue hotel, not worth emptying until it overflows.

In the early 1970s a strange cult arose—the spray-painting of names, numbers, primitive slogans and flamboyant designs on and in buses and subway trains. This could be interpreted as the strangled cry of men crushed by the megalopolis and seeking identity; some of the graffiti were taken seriously by students of sociology as representing a new art-form rebelling against the circumambient ugliness created by city planners, property developers and powerful corporations. In fact, very little of Manhattan's ugliness is the work of big men who care nothing for the amenities of the masses; it is, rather, the creation of ordinary citizens, who themselves tend to treat their city as a *thing*, not as a living organism—a thing for using, exploiting, maltreating, never cherishing.

I see that I am being hard on New Yorkers. Yet my recollection of individual New Yorkers does not conduce to such hard words. When I remember them I am often vague about their racial origin, which is perhaps a terrible affront to them. To me, it is the New Yorkness in them that matters. It is the demotic New York voice that stays in my mind more than faces and the colour of faces—firm, clear, fairly slow, the tone-pattern various and somewhat querulous, ready for the dogmatic utterance that trembles on the verge of an epigram or wisecrack, world-wise, resigned, incapable of registering new surprise, capable of unexpected courtesy, neutral but warily prepared to be friendly.

I asked a cab-driver to take me to 666, Fifth Avenue, please, and he said "Thank you". Why that "thank you", I wanted to know. "Because ya said 'please'," he replied. I remember the cab-driver who picked me up in Brooklyn and took me, at my request, to a very low dive in Spanish Harlem. While I was on my first drink, I noticed him, quiet and unobtrusive, near me, ordering a stein. He felt, he said, responsible for me, a stranger in the dangerous city, and wanted to stay by. No big gestures, not many words, but a lot of good will.

I have found plenty of this, and even when ill will has been thrown at me—through a letter or telephone call—it has always been possible to interpret it as a kind of concern. If, in London, I make a television statement or write an article of provocative content, I feel I am casting my words into a great silence. Not so in New York. I made a slight error in a university lecture. Lecture and error alike were publicized in *The New York Times* and the flood of letters and calls could hardly be coped with. This kind of concern, not uncommon in a small English village, is not to be found in any other great city of the world. It is an aspect of the latent neighbourliness of New York, and it totally contradicts the go-getting egocentrism I have just presented.

Few New Yorkers, however, will actually admit to the possession of lovable qualities, since, if they have them, other New Yorkers probably have them too, and that notion is hardly to be tolerated. Fewer still will admit to loving their city. This may have something to do with the lack of cataclysmic civic experience—the kind of experience that elsewhere imposes a feeling of civic unity. London, for example, had its Great Fire in 1666 and its blitz during the Second World War. God forbid that New York should ever be blitzed, but sometimes only the knowledge of an enemy without can compel an urgent sense of brotherhood within.

As may be expected, New Yorkers do best in times of crisis. If the police are on strike, the criminals, in sympathy, go on strike too—if the subways don't run, motorists are generous with lifts. The notorious East Coast blackout of 1965 actually reduced the crime figures for that night. At Christmas there is a huge Dickensian burst of benevolence. At other times, alas, fear and indifference compel New Yorkers to watch their fellow-citizens being mugged or even killed without moving a muscle to help. The urge to earn a living and look after their own repels the wider civic— meaning, the deeper human—sense. West 93rd Street and Yorkville may beget communities of friends, but New York is too often a city full of strangers.

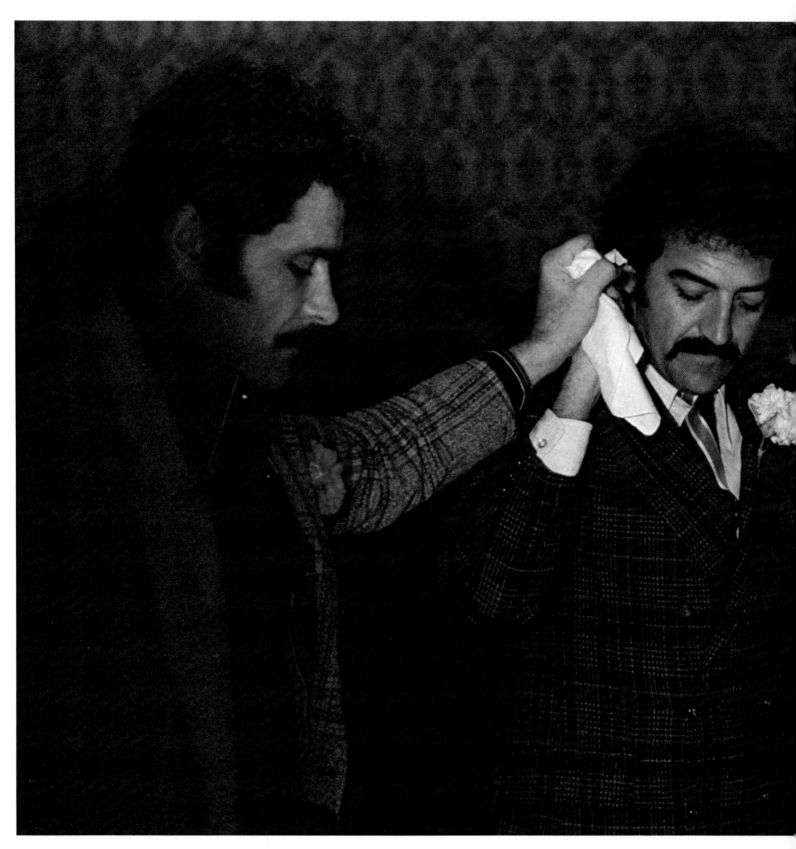

A City of Many Lands

PHOTOGRAPHS BY ENRICO FERORELLI

At a wedding on Manhattan's West Side, some of the city's 350,000-strong community of Greeks perform a dance that recalls the traditions of their homeland.

New York, so often termed a "melting pot", is really no such thing. It has never entirely homogenized its constituent groups. It is still—as it always was—a sociological cauldron of races, nationalities, religions, interests and classes. In 1870, more than half the population was of foreign stock; today, the proportion is still almost as great, although there have been changes in the elements that compose the mix. Major groups include the long-established Italians, Irish and Jews; small, tight-knit enclaves of Greeks (above) and Chinese; and the more recently-swollen numbers of Caribbean newcomers. The balance shifts constantly as neighbourhoods that were once the domain of one group become the home of another— often undergoing in the process a change that stamps upon them the look and colour of an exotic culture.

His mixed culture shown by his clothes, a Chinese-American pauses by a mural of Chinese life in America.

Oriental Manhattan

Chinatown, a few blocks in south Manhattan, was notoriously violent in the early 1900s:
a corner of Doyers Street is known as Bloody Angle in memory of gang murders committed
there. Now it is a thriving, largely peaceful community, a haunt for tourists charmed by its
restaurants with their long, inexpensive menus, its ideogrammatic newstands, its pagoda
telephone booths and its annual New Year parade, complete with papier mache dragon.

Children of Chinese origin practise the calligraphy they will need to help them absorb the traditions of their 100,000 culture- and family-conscious kinsfolk.

Decorated telephone booths in Chinatown look exotic with their pointed roofs, but the Chinese characters convey a simple meaning: "Public Telephone".

In a traditional Jewish enclave—the Williamsburg section of Brooklyn—an elderly Orthodox Jew passes the window of a shop selling Jewish religious items.

Hats, sombre black dress, and uncut ringlets distinguish two Hasidic Jews.

A Corner of Old Europe

Around 1900, the Jews were, with the Italians, the poor of the city. Mostly impoverished Eastern Europeans, they soon rose out of the ghettos in which they had settled; many are now prosperous businessmen and professionals. But small pockets persist, where black-clad elders lead lives not far different from those of their forebears in the old country.

The Spanish Touch

Since 1945, waves of migrants from Puerto Rico have swelled the city's Hispanic contingent to more than one tenth of the total population, and Spanish has become the city's second language. They have brought with them their own traditions and their rhythmic music—and into the city's gastronomic melting pot they have stirred many of Puerto Rico's tropical fruits and vegetables.

At an East Harlem market stall a black woman sells statuettes and other ornaments which reveal a Puerto Rican brand of Catholicism tinged with spiritualism.

This shop in Little Italy displays two florid national symbols—Mussolini and Sophia Loren.

Little Italy

Until the 1920s, Italians—mainly southern peasants—flowed by the thousands into New York, a mainstream of poor and dispossessed. The one and a half million Italians now in the city still retain the close family and village groups of their homeland. Families may prosper, but they do not move easily, and neighbourhoods endure. Here, youthful gangs and groups of older men preserve their fathers' male-dominant traditions that still prevail in the Old World.

In Manhattan's Washington Square, near the section called Little Italy, young and old Italian-Americans play bocci, a type of bowls, traditional in Italy.

3

All Around the Town

My first visit to New York was touristy and Algonquin-coddled and confined to a few blocks around Times Square. My second was more, or less, adventurous. I was doing some work at Long Island University and was housed in Brooklyn, that vast bag of territory that is bounded by Queens to the north and east, the East River and New York Bay and the Narrows to the west, and the Atlantic to the south. I was in a bar one day, sheltering from the knifing February winds of the East River, and struck up with an old man, who said without preamble:

"Okay, professor, what happened in 1883?"

"Richard Wagner died," I said. It was true, but the wrong answer.

"What happened in 1883," said the old man, "was that they finished building the bridge. Before that we was cut off from them bastards over there. It was the beginning of the end. Brooklyn getting all fouled up with City Hall politics. And we used to be free. Independent."

I had not expected such fierce local patriotism, but I can understand it now. Brooklyn is not alone in resenting Manhattan; Queens, the Bronx and Staten Island are all capable of voicing a historical grouse against the predatory reachings out of the cocky little island of Manhattan. It all began after the Civil War, when Manhattan wanted to become not merely a city but a metropolis. The reunited States already had a capital, Washington, so Manhattan, the nucleus of Greater New York, would have to be content with world rather than national stature. Hence the clamour to expand laterally, to send out tentacles over—and under—the waterways to enmesh what are now the other boroughs of the city. It was done, and is still being done, with bridges and tunnels.

The old man in the Brooklyn bar had his date right. Although the incorporation of his city, along with Queens County and Staten Island, into Greater New York (the Bronx had already been annexed) did not occur until 1898, the Brooklyn Bridge was completed in 1883.

This engineering masterpiece, which took 13 years to build, rammed home the political significance of its construction by connecting the City Hall area of Manhattan with the Borough Hall area of Brooklyn. The latest of the great New York bridges, the Verrazano-Narrows, which linked Brooklyn to Staten Island in 1964, should, by 1883 standards, have taken 32 years to complete, since it is two-and-a-half times longer. Actually it took five. The water city had become expert, in the period since 1883, in throwing up bridges—the Throgs Neck, the Triborough, the Bronx Whitestone, the Queensboro, the Hell Gate, the Manhattan, the Williamsburg, the

In an organized tangle of coiling access-roads the east-west Cross Bronx Expressway intersects with the north-south Major Deegan Expressway, on the Bronx side of the narrow Harlem River (background). A complete circulatory system of these great arterial routes, with 17 major bridges and tunnels, connects New York's five boroughs into one sprawling organism.

Alexander Hamilton, the Henry Hudson, the Marine Parkway, the Cross Bay Boulevard, the Bayonne, and all the others. Manhattan has grappled the subsidiary boroughs to herself with arms of Bessemer steel.

Subsidiary? Brooklyn is a great city in its own right, with a population of some three million, and yet Manhattan thinks of it as a mere appendage. Workers stream across the Brooklyn Bridge—as well as the more recent Manhattan and Williamsburg Bridges, and through the Brooklyn Battery Tunnel and the subway tunnels—to the arrogant little centre of the world and then, tired, stream back again. "You must understand," Dickens confided to a friend, "that Brooklyn is a kind of sleeping-place for New York, and is supposed to be a great place in the money way." Brooklyn is also full of churches and they say it is a good place to die.

On Brooklyn's sea-washed southern edge there are Manhattan Beach and Coney Island. "Coney Island," wrote an English visitor in 1881, "is a rather fast, jolly, rollicking place, and serves its purpose well, as the health-breathing lungs of a great city." Many fastidious middle-class New Yorkers nowadays find it neither jolly nor rollicking, but to my mind it remains a true fun city. I have taken the Sea Beach Express and got off at Stillwell Avenue to swim and to eat hot dogs (the best, the original) and affirm that mankind, in summer undress, is both lovable and insufferable. I have been to the Aquarium and seen the whales and penguins and sharks. I have also seen the Brooklyn Botanic Garden, and consider that these two are among the great places of America.

More serious things are also to be observed here. The terrifying contrasts of elegance and squalor, of wealth and abysmal poverty, that Brooklyn shares with its neighbour over the water are not accepted as an unchangeable endowment of Nature. Nobody—Brooklyner or visitor—can remain unmoved by the clash between the relative affluence of Brooklyn Heights, which takes as its due the superb view of the Manhattan skyline and harbour, and the agony of Brownsville, a slum that can hardly find a parallel in the Old World.

Naples is slummy but picturesque. Brownsville is a wretched patch of carious buildings, dead shops, filthy tenements, dejection, alienation, families with little or no income, unenlivened by the sordid gaiety of the old East End of London. Brooklyn has a black community of about half a million, spread over the area south-east of Long Island University in a strip leading from Bedford-Stuyvesant to the rock-bottom of Brownsville, and the problems here are so immense that they just have to enforce action.

Brooklyn also matches Manhattan in its racial variety. In Crown Heights two groups with little in common except a myth of bondage and hope of deliverance have been ferociously working together to clear slums and provide decent, cheap housing. I mean that the Jews are in harness with the blacks. In Brooklyn the Jews are a powerful civic force, exhibiting—especially in Borough Park—a powerful orthodoxy that disdains the mere

Brooklyn Bridge has a history as dramatic as its silhouette. Its designer, John Roebling, died after an accident on the site. His son, Washington Roebling, as chief engineer, was also injured during construction, but for 12 years oversaw operations from his sickbed until the span was completed in 1883. Later the bridge became a favoured point for suicide leaps.

show of architectural religiosity. There are synagogues here that look like shops. The Italians mostly keep to themselves, chiefly in Bensonhurst—south of Borough Park, towards Gravesend Bay—where they literally cultivate their own gardens. Here there is even a settlement of Mohawk Indians who have exploited an old tribal tradition of cool nerves into traditional employment on high rising construction projects, such as the Verrazano-Narrows Bridge.

Brooklyn is Manhattan-like, too, in its organized crime (East New York, part of Brooklyn, was the home of Murder Inc., the band of professional killers that enforced the dictates of the big-time racketeers throughout the United States between 1930 and 1940) and in its commercial bustle. Large factories lie scattered along the waterfront, and great vessels—although not so many as there used to be—lie on the water: to cross the Atlantic from New York is often to sail from Brooklyn. Although it fails in glamour—even the borough's baseball team, the Brooklyn Dodgers, left Brooklyn's Flatbush section for Los Angeles in 1957—Brooklyn is evidently not short on creative vigour. There is a neighbourly charm about those streets, named for flowers and trees and fruit, and an inviting cosiness about the little dive bars where I used to spend some of my afternoons. There is solidity, but also concern; not too much neurosis and not too much respectability.

North and east of Brooklyn is Queens, no mean borough with its population of two million and still growing. Queens is to too many visitors merely the place where John F. Kennedy International Airport flaunts its numberless sundered terminals—or where La Guardia Airport connects New York with the rest of the nation. But Queens has many earthbound distinctions, most of which sprang from a desire to be respectable, bourgeois, unchanging, immune from the contagion of Manhattan life.

It is, among other things, a borough of refugees from decay and decline —decent people who have moved out of Manhattan or Brooklyn or the Bronx, unwilling either to tolerate or to fight urban deterioration there, who now find the problem has pursued them into their supposed sanctuary. While Manhattan's population dropped in the 1960s, that of Queens rose by nearly a quarter of a million. This meant, and still means, rapidly run-up apartment blocks and jerry-built, low-price housing projects and an influx of low-income families, all of which the older inhabitants of Queens resent and resist. They live in their own houses, many of them. This, surprisingly and hearteningly, means the blacks as well as the whites.

I have not yet met a man in a Queens bar prepared to extol the greatness and beauty of the borough as a whole. There is, in fact, a lot to boast about. Poverty and slums exist, but there is also the Forest Hills Tennis Stadium, and in Shea Stadium the Jets play football and the Mets play baseball. There are Forest Park and Kissena Park and Oakland Gardens. There are also the fine beaches of the Rockaways, and the Jamaica Bay Wildlife Refuge, the largest urban reserve in the world, fringes Kennedy.

Nevertheless, it is still difficult for a Queens dweller to look outside his immediate neighbourhood with much interest, and probably this is an instance of history getting in the way. While Brooklyn was an independent township at the time of the merger of 1898, Queens—established as a

Onward and Outward

In Manhattan's teeming centre, space is at a premium; people are crowded and rents high. But New York gradually relaxes as it spreads out. Buildings are smaller and the pace of life slower. Green replaces concrete; gardens, cramped at first, grow more ample as the pressure on space lessens. The progression is illustrated by this series of aerial photographs which swings in an arc from midtown Manhattan over to Brooklyn and Queens. The luxurious Long Island homes of wealthy families, embowered in park-like surroundings (far right), provide the culmination to the series—a dream for some New Yorkers, but anathema to others who need the stimulation and excitement offered by Manhattan.

Manhattan's East 60s   **Streets in Brooklyn**

county in the 17th Century and named in honour of Charles II's wife, Catherine of Braganza—was a loose group of villages (the eastern ones chose to resist the grasp of centralizing Manhattan and formed Nassau County). In many ways, it still is.

Go to Woodside, south-west of La Guardia, and you will find an Irish community of fantastic conservatism. Astoria—named for John Jacob Astor, the fur trader, who died in 1848 the wealthiest man in America—lies north-west of Woodside and looks on to the East River. It is second in Greek population only to Greece itself. The Corona district is richly and aromatically Italian and can indulge in ancestor-worship on its own ground, not just "back home" in near mythical Naples or Palermo.

The Bronx, the borough north of Manhattan, is about one-third the size of Queens, but it is home to at least a million and a half people. Enclosed by Long Island Sound, the Hudson, East and Harlem Rivers, and Westchester County (it is thus the only part of New York City to touch the American mainland), it lacks the spaciousness of Queens and, to the student of urban change, it is both more frightening and more exciting. It is the home of Yankee Stadium, and its contribution to American mythology has been chiefly the "Bronx cheer"—a resounding raspberry. But it is capable of evil and squalor as well as vulgarity.

In the South Bronx and Hunt's Point, where drug addicts and pushers abound, there are vistas of abandoned warehouses and burned-out tenements. Whole communities seek to end their misery in a kind of social suicide. Tenants set their own decrepit buildings ablaze to guarantee priority access to municipal housing elsewhere. Firemen have found cans

Outer Brooklyn homes   **Garden streets in Queens**   **Long Island woodlands**

Although nine miles away, the unmistakable towers of Manhattan's World Trade Center are so high that they dominate even these comfortable waterside homes at Sheepshead Bay in the suburbs of south Brooklyn.

of fuel left by the arsonists and baths weighted with bricks to ensure that joists collapse. In spite of an industrious 80 miles of waterfront, a great zoo, the campus of Fordham University and the green expanse of Van Cortlandt Park, nothing halts the spread of poverty and violence and the exodus of middle-income citizens.

There is also racial strife in the Bronx. The Puerto Rican population is growing fast, and it is contending with the black element for political power. Herman Badillo, the first Puerto Rican borough president in the history of New York City, was elected in the Bronx in 1965 and he became at length a U.S. Congressman. There are Puerto Ricans in the state legislature at Albany, all trained in Bronx borough politics. The political action is concerned with stopping the spread of slums, strangling drug-pushing and related crimes, and keeping the citizens of the Bronx within their proper borough by promoting middle-income housing developments in salubrious surroundings. It is heartening to see so much action in the hands of an ethnic group as traditionally "deprived" as the Puerto Ricans.

The last of the boroughs is Staten Island, the name of which is derived from the 17th-Century Dutch States General or *Staten-General*. It lies to the south of Manhattan and is separated from the rest of the city by New York Bay and the Narrows, and from New Jersey by the pencil-thin Arthur Kill and Kill Van Kull channels. The nearness of Staten Island to New Jersey, and the ligatures made with that state through several bridges, have always made it seem very remote and rural to Manhattan, with which it makes connection by the romantic Staten Island ferry.

A ride on this is perhaps the most restful of New York's pleasures, granting a fine view of the Statue of Liberty, Governor's Island, and Ellis

Lit by a rosy blush from the east, the focal spire of the Empire State Building presides over both the skyline of central Manhattan and the quiet stones of St. John's graveyard in the borough of Queens.

Island, once the immigrant's gate to the Union, as well as downtown New York's spectacular skyline. The ferry ride was long known as the world's best bargain and may still be, even though the traditional five cent fare, introduced in 1886, was in 1975 at last raised to 35 cents.

That means of transport is now being severely strained as the population of Staten Island—once the most sparsely inhabited of all the boroughs—steadily grows. The open country is being built upon rapidly, and the urbanization is random, ugly, higgledy-piggledy. The opening in 1964 of the Verrazano-Narrows Bridge, which ties Staten Island to Brooklyn, has had a great deal to do with this, as has also the frantic search on the part of so many New Yorkers for a refuge from slums and violence. Real-estate speculators seek quick profits, and conscientious Staten Islanders fight against the loss of rural amenity. Too many woodlands are under the axe and too many meadows are vanishing under brick.

There is industry enough on Staten Island—shipbuilding, oil refining, metallurgy—and plenty of history. With permission from Manhattan's Dutch rulers, French Waldenses and Huguenots came here in the 1660s to help thicken the stew of New York religious life. It was the Conference House in Tottenville, on the island's southern tip, that saw the final breakdown of talks between the British and the Americans after the Battle of Long Island in 1776. The Staten Island Historical Society Museum has restored several pre-Revolutionary buildings, including the Voolezer's House, believed to be the oldest elementary schoolhouse in the United States, and plans to restore other buildings.

The boroughs are bound together physically with bridges, road tunnels, railways, subways. Binding them together politically has always been more difficult, and one wonders whether it can really be done. During the financial and political crisis of the mid-1970s only two ways of preserving the city from collapse seemed to present themselves to the city's political leaders. These, being respectively more centralization and less, proved, of course, impossible to reconcile. The conflict was nothing new. Manhattan, metropolis of the metropolis, argued as far back as 1930 that a centralized bureaucracy, controlling such utilities as education, sanitation, roads and parks, was a more efficient and economical engine than one that replicated the same offices from borough to borough. It was recognized that each borough had a right to its president; but it was also recognized, not without protest, that the real power should be lodged with the Mayor of New York City—whom the boroughs could not help seeing as really the mayor of Manhattan—and the officials he appointed.

The 1960s, with the glamorous Mayor John Lindsay in office, saw the rumble of protest against centralization grow to something of a roar. The burden of outcry was expected and traditional: the city's government was cut off from the people's needs, the essential functions of city organization were being neglected—streets in disrepair, rubbish uncollected, slums slow

Two little boys—proud possessors of an ice-hockey set—practise a roller-skate version of the game on the spick-and-span sidewalks of Manhattan's privileged Upper East Side, beside Central Park. The outline of a West Side apartment building rises in the distance.

to be cleared, violence and robbery on the increase. Only local community-planning boards, it was argued, had done something about such horrors as the Brownsville slums in Brooklyn, the strengthening of the police force in areas notoriously lawless, the re-equipping of fire stations in a city always plagued by fires, preventing the wanton throwing up of new department stores in residential districts, rehousing welfare cases.

Although the Mayor and his City Planning Commissioners complain loudly that local pressures obstruct the work of the central administration, it is still the local community that commands local loyalties. Anyone coming from Europe to live in New York is aware of the almost fanatical degree of social consciousness that can operate even in communities as small as the apartment block, especially when it is generated among intellectual Jews. Such a living unit can have its own magazine, its own uniform for its own armed guard, its own political, social and cultural officers.

When I first moved into an apartment on Manhattan's West End Avenue I had to be screened—but also wined and dined—by the appropriate block committee, which was naturally anxious to know whether I was sufficiently clean, civilized and responsible. Committee meetings and block parties would be convened to deal with new problems of security and even street cleanliness. When I wrote an article in *The New York Times* mentioning the prevalence of cockroaches—not complaining, actually glorying in them as a sort of vigorous, poor alternative Manhattan complete with their own literary voice, *Archy*, created by poet Don Marais—I was attacked as a man letting down the side. I like this local patriotism. It is not to be found to anything near the same extent in London.

Neighbourliness is, I think, the right term for New York, and it is found at its most piquant in Manhattan. After all, this borough which is not even a city complete in itself contrives to be the capital of the world, and yet it resolves itself into a bundle of neighbourhoods.

Manhattan can be seen from a tour bus, from a boat that circles the island in three hours, or, for visitors who prefer spectacular views to intimate ones, from a sightseeing helicopter. But the mix of languages cannot be heard from a helicopter and the aromas of exotic cooking cannot be sniffed from an air-conditioned touring bus. The only way to absorb the flavours of Manhattan's neighbourhoods is to explore them on foot. I literally have walked for days in Manhattan—not, I should say, non-stop—and for present purposes I shall string some of those strolls together into a continuous tour around the island.

If we begin where I lived on the Upper West Side—West 93rd Street—and walk north along Broadway, we are soon in Puerto Rican territory, with Spanish notices on the walls and a shoeshop owner telling me: *"No hay zapatos para gringos"* (which means, approximately, "There are no shoes here for Anglos," although "gringos" loses its intended element of disparagement when translated to Anglos). But this is a fine neighbour-

Firemen tackle an out-of-control blaze in the South Bronx. In this poverty-stricken section of New York, arson is so rampant that fires have averaged 33 a night. Among the fire-raisers are tenants who put the match to their own apartments hoping to be rehoused by the city—and landlords, who, beset by problems of high taxes and low rents, seek to escape the burden of ownership.

hood to be in if you are seeking the academic life rather than footwear, for here are Columbia University, its chiefly feminine affiliate, Barnard College, the Jewish Theological Seminary, and (long live New York religious diversity) directly across the street the Union Theological Seminary, a training ground for Protestant clergy. To a Mancunian like myself, who went to Manchester University daily through streets full of fights and brothels, there is nothing very disconcerting about finding a college in a world of slums, even when the slums are Harlem.

The original Haarlem in Holland means something to Haarlem dwellers only, but this Harlem is not only a home to many New York blacks —and rather fewer Puerto Ricans and Italians—but a universal word of fear and shame and other emotions. Crammed, but in many cases also damnably expensive, Harlem's dilapidated old tenement houses form a blot that spreads across Manhattan island north of Central Park and through the conscience of America. A scattering of new housing projects does very little to mitigate the squalor. But Harlem has a verve, vigour and popular cultural tradition that set it well above Bedford Stuyvesant, Brownsville and the South Bronx, which rival or even surpass it in blight.

If Harlem is too depressing or too unwelcoming (as I have said, white strangers do not meet a warm reception there), one may go west to the bank of the Hudson River, where a slender strip of green runs all the way to the island's northern tip. It is not one park but a series of them: Riverside, Sheltering Arms, Fort Washington, Fort Tryon and Inwood Hill Parks, an admirable dedication of valuable urban land to Nature which would be more admirable still did not a six-lane motorway slice all the way up the middle of it. The views of the elegant George Washington suspension bridge and the stony cliffs of New Jersey are some compensation for the pervading miasma of automobile exhaust fumes.

There are other compensations too. In Fort Tryon Park a monastery-like museum, The Cloisters, invites New Yorkers and visitors to look at medieval art. If the wanderer does not find that surprising, perhaps neither will he be astonished to discover that Inwood, Manhattan's northernmost community, is full of Irish pubs, hurling, Gaelic football, vilification of the British, healthful punch-ups and other Hibernian sports.

We return south along the Harlem and East Rivers to the opposite side of Central Park from where we began. This is the Upper East Side, very chic, very expensive, with an abundance of trees, smart art galleries, and brownstones (which in New York often means any terraced houses, of brown stone or not). Here there are palatial mansions costing half a million dollars occupied by the rich and famous, and tiny, thin-walled apartments full of secretaries and young executives amid the trappings of a modish "singles" lifestyle.

An even wider contrast of high and low living standards is found in the East 80s in a neighbourhood known as Yorkville. But here the stratification

A quaint addition to Greenwich Village's varied scene is this 18th-Century house which, in 1967, was moved in toto to its new location from its original site on Manhattan's upper East Side. Its owners, not wishing to see it razed by developers, had the 12-ton, six-room house loaded on to a wheeled platform and rolled through the streets to its present address.

of wealth is unified by the German language and much adherence to Old World German cultural values. Yorkville has a coherence, stability and relatively low crime rate that make it the envy of generally classier neighbourhoods in this neurotic city. But neurosis, although an *echt* Viennese property, accords ill with devotion to the old German bourgeois culture, and Yorkville's sanity owes much to its spurning of modernity. One might add that it is graced, at the eastern end of 86th Street, by Gracie Mansion, an 18th-Century dwelling where the Mayor of New York lives elegantly embowered in the green of Carl Schurz Park.

We walk south along Park Avenue, the Manhattan success story made manifest in stone, glass and a most untypical cleanliness. North of 96th Street, Park Avenue is low, undignified and slummy, but from there it moves majestically south, at first between some of New York's priciest apartment buildings and later into a wide canyon of glass-sheathed office blocks, until it is seemingly terminated at 46th Street by Grand Central Terminal and the towering Pan Am Building which sit athwart it.

Beyond this agglomeration of structures the avenue actually resumes its course, but that part of it is marginally less glamorous. There may be a moral—something to do with the tenuousness of all New York wealth and glamour—in the fact that the part of Park Avenue that glistens most brightly with money and class is not on the firm face of the earth but on the roof of railway tracks that run north from Grand Central station.

To the west of Park Avenue—beyond that other myth-laden thoroughfare, Madison Avenue—lies the street that represents the apotheosis of the art of retail selling: Fifth Avenue. There is a Fifth Avenue Association

(Inc.) that not only promotes present amenity and profit but marvels poetically that, where now the Empire State Building stands, woodcock and partridge drummed in the thickets, snipe were shot, mink, otter and muskrat lurked in the ponds and marshes.

That there was once a natural world in place of the glass and concrete never ceases to cause wonder to New Yorkers, those great existentialists to whom history is a cinematic dream. Even New York's Crystal Palace—which stood where the Public Library now stands on Fifth Avenue and burnt out prematurely in 1858, almost a whole century before its London prototype burned—is mixed into myth that might as well be Homeric. For the existential reality is the vista of shop windows artfully cluttered with some of the world's most expensive merchandise, including diamond necklaces, fashionable gowns and stuffed toy animals several times the size of the small children for whom they are intended and therefore large enough to reflect prestige on the purchasing father's bank balance.

A long walk to the south-east takes us into a very different neighbourhood indeed, the Bowery. (The name commemorates Peter Stuyvesant's bouwerie, or farm, and the dusty remains of the old Dutchman himself lie near by in the graveyard of St. Mark's-in-the-Bouwerie church on Second Avenue.) Since the late 19th Century the Bowery has been a desolation of dosshouses and pawnshops, the prostrate alcoholic, the Bowery Bum—Skid Row. Urban redevelopment has transformed some of the area.

But in America, thanks to the hunger of the cinema industry, most institutions turn into myth, and the myth tries self-consciously to maintain itself. The *Bowery News* thus called itself "The Voice of Society's Basement" and the bum cried hallelujah at his own sordid glamour—especially when a coachload of tourists was passing. Near by, the decay of the old Lower East Side, full of poverty, Yiddish, wretched tenements, pushcart vendors, a place from whose steamy darkness men who later became rich and famous first fought towards the light, is proving even more resistant to the planners.

We walk south to South Street and follow it south-west along the pier-lined East River waterfront. The Fulton Fish Market used to be here. Its pungent stench of wet, fresh-caught fish, a kind of olfactory landmark that once was loved by many New Yorkers, has now vanished, for the market has yielded to redevelopment and our nostrils are assailed by the exhaust fumes of cars roaring along the elevated highway over our heads. Only if compelled by public outcry to do so will New York cling to the old.

Past the terminal where the Staten Island ferry starts and returns, we reach the Battery. This is where New York began—where the Dutch allegedly made their now famous $24 real-estate purchase from the Algonquin Indians—and, appropriately, here, at least, some of old New York has been preserved. Castle Clinton, a fort built at the beginning of the 19th Century and named after Governor DeWitt Clinton, still stands in

New York apartment-dwellers yearning for
Nature manage to cultivate a surprising amount
of greenery—and in the most surprising places.
High above Park Avenue, a man proudly shows
off a roof garden that he employs three
professional gardeners to tend.

Battery Park (the federal government made it a national monument so New York could not tear it down). Across the street from the park the oval-shaped Bowling Green still has the iron fence that was built around it in 1771. Colonists used to pay a single peppercorn a year for the privilege of playing bowls here. In those days there was a statue of George III by the green, but when the War of Independence began New Yorkers melted it down and made it into cannonballs to fire at George's ships.

On this southernmost end of the island high finance and big government jostling for space have squeezed out most mementoes of the past. But a few survive in the shadows of skyscraper bank headquarters and city and federal offices. One can still pray in Trinity Church at the Broadway end of Wall Street, a few steps from the Stock Exchange which has supplanted it as the prime centre of worship for many New Yorkers. And Fraunces Tavern, where George Washington bade farewell to his officers at the end of the War of Independence, still offers food and drink, as well as history, at the corner of Broad and Pearl Streets.

One thing a visitor from London notices at once about this entire area— including the financial district, City Hall, the state, city and federal courts, the Tombs prison and police headquarters—is the fact that it is not cut off, after the day's work, from aromatic humanity. In London, the City is dead after the long day of trading and administration, but here a vital neighbourhood is growing up near City Hall and the temples of money. Some old streets of historic character have been restored and new blocks have gone up along the East River.

To the north, abutting on the Bowery, is Chinatown, where as recently as the 1920s there was sanguinary warfare between rival tongs, organizations which then were not all that different in purpose or activity from today's criminal Mafia families. A sharp bend in Doyers Street which lent itself to ambush became known as the Bloody Angle, so many killings took place there—more, said the police, than in any other single spot on the face of the earth. And the air was filled with the scent of opium smoke.

Today one looks elsewhere for murder or drugs. The tongs support their members' widows, and crime is a rarity. Instead Chinatown sells Chinese culture, jade trinkets and Chinese cuisine, conforming to the ethos of a city where everything is for sale. You can buy Chinoiserie even when making a call from the pagoda-shaped telephone booths.

In New York, profitably selling your culture is one way of fending off the planners. And so we come to Greenwich Village, to whose residents— genuine students and self-styled artists, although occasionally the other way round—planners are anathema. In the Village the Euclidian geometry of New York breaks down. The streets are not straight and, according to popular conception, neither are the residents. In Manhattan generally streets are supposed to run east and west and avenues north and south. But if you are seeking a location in the Village carry a map, because there are several onomastic anomalies. West 10th Street crosses West Fourth Street, for instance; Greenwich Street and Greenwich Avenue run roughly parallel courses; and some distance above West 12th Street you will find Little West 12th Street.

As for the people, I am not inclined to regard the Village as more than a pocket of fringe artiness. Its great creative names belong mainly to the past. Washington Irving and Thomas Paine lived here, as did Theodore Dreiser and Eugene O'Neill. John Masefield mopped the floor of a Village tavern (needless to say, before he become England's Poet Laureate) and the Welsh poet Dylan Thomas drank himself to death in another (The White Horse Tavern at 11th and Hudson Streets). The village became Bohemian (blessed, vague term) somewhat by accident, since its older destiny led to Henry James rather than to a nameless, hairy poetling ranting free verse in a coffee house.

Henry James memorialized Washington Square with its beautiful neo-Grecian homes, the epicentre of Village intellectual tremors. As in London's Mayfair, its stables became mews addresses for struggling artists, but these have become expensive and perhaps only thoroughbred horses could afford them. Unknown to most of the folk-singers with guitars who serenade the public there, it was once a place of public executions, where until 1828 New York hanged many of its wrongdoers and buried them. To walk across the Square is to tread on hundreds of graves.

Then the Village was a rustic haven for New Yorkers fleeing from the epidemics of yellow fever and cholera that periodically struck the city. Nowadays the Village is invaded by tourists and midtown executives playing at being weekend bohemians (all eagerly reading the weekly *Village Voice*, which has steadily become a pillar of near-establishment journalism).

These, in turn, have driven out hungry writers and painters and assorted denizens of the so-called Alternative Society who colonized near-by areas where rents were cheaper. In the slums east of Fourth Avenue they established what became the East Village. Other refugees from soaring Greenwich Village housing costs moved south of Houston Street into a neighbourhood called—with acronymic simplicity and perhaps just a nod towards London's one-time centre of Bohemian life— SoHo, *So*uth of *Ho*uston Street. SoHo's authentic odour of artistic endeavour may be aerosolled out, like that of the mother Village, as more and more expensive restaurants and fancy galleries open there and the pseudo-fringe moves in. Greenwich Village, to give the place its due, has always been more than its Bohemian associations. It includes its own Little Italy, centred on Bleecker Street, and it is exalted by New York University and blessed by a great number of churches. It is a micropolis with its own *moeurs* and culture, an aesthetic and intellectual feeder of the megalopolis, and it has tried, in its oblique way, to impress its independence and uniqueness on potential planners, who would gladly knock down its

On a typical neighbourhood playground in Spanish Harlem, paved over and wire-netted, local youths play a pickup game of basketball—called "the city's game".

scruffy bedsitters and studies and fill the space with high-rises. The true villager is powerfully aware that his sprawling enclave has a soul of its own.

Moving north from the Village we find, where Broadway meets Sixth Avenue at 34th Street, two triangles known as squares—Herald Square and Greeley Square, the first named for the old *New York Herald* and the other for Horace Greeley, founder of the *New York Tribune*. The two journals merged in 1924 to become the New York *Herald Tribune*, one of the world's great newspapers until it died in New York (a European edition is still published) in 1966, which may be taken to indicate that New Yorkers once thought more highly of their Press than they do nowadays.

I mention these two squares not for their interest to the history of journalism, however, but because here the world of great department stores begins—Macy's, its two million square feet of floor space supporting its claim to be one of the largest on earth, at Herald Square, and its equally famous rival, Gimbel Brothers, at Greeley Square. To the west, the garment district that feeds these stores—and those of the rest of the nation—spreads itself along Seventh Avenue, emerging on to the streets in a flurry of furs and a minced-up rainbow of dresses.

Where Seventh Avenue and Broadway meet—between 42nd and 47th Streets—is another set of triangles. New Yorkers call the whole area Times Square (named for *The New York Times*, which once occupied the building that stands at the south end of it). Properly the northern triangle is called Duffy Square, if you wish to get one up on residents who are ignorant of that distinction. Times Square is a centre of light, colour and decayed glamour, the place people often mean when they refer to Broadway since this is where many of the theatres are.

It is the place George M. Cohan certainly meant when he wrote the song, *Give My Regards to Broadway*, and it is where Cohan's statue stands. Broadway as the Great White Way of theatres requires a chapter to itself, and the less said about other aspects of this area, the better, especially the 42nd Street end of it, which is a mess of strip-joints, hard-core pornshops, pornflickdens, inferior pizza parlours and over-amplified rock-music that strikes like neuralgia.

After a short stroll to the north, amenity improves at Central Park South, which is the name given to that part of 59th Street that forms the southern boundary of Central Park, Manhattan's great green lung, which is available for everyone's healthful aeration by day, and by night, the quietus of the ignorant or unwary. Here we find some of America's grandest hotels, including the Plaza, one of the grandest of all, and, facing them from the park, an array of monuments. Columbus himself is here. So is General Sherman, the man who led the march through Georgia during the Civil War. And so is Simon Bolivar, the liberator of South America from Spanish colonialism, who holds the same place in the hearts of Spanish-speaking New Yorkers as does George Washington in the hearts of those who speak English. Let it be noted that Bolivar's monument was erected before Spanish speakers became a strong political power in the city. It was inspired by New York homage to liberty in general rather than to Puerto Rican voters in particular.

From here we stroll westwards up Broadway, making the occasional excursion farther west yet to West End Avenue and Riverside Drive. We find a world where luxury and squalor live together. The square-set apartment blocks were built in the 1920s and 1930s to house the coming generation of the wealthy and the fashionable. The entrance halls are capacious, many of them displaying artistry and some of them dignity.

But Wealth and Fashion chose the East Side, and the West Side—except for a narrow band along the park, where apartments in remarkably fine old mansion blocks with views of greenery remain the exclusive preserve of the well-to-do—became a medley of peoples. Long established Jewish matriarchs gaze out over nodding junkies and restaurants that proclaim Spanish-Chinese cuisine. The combination of space and relative cheapness has also made the area a lure for professionals with young families. They are not the traditional executive conformists with button-down shirts, close-shaves and sculptured haircuts. Jeaned, sweatered, tousled, fervidly involved, they have invigorated countless committees, block associations, school boards and hospital administrations.

We are back where we began. There are two kinds of life in New York—one ethnic, one supraethnic—and in this jammed city neither can be sealed off from the other. No neighbourhood is isolated in total cultural purity. Two professors from Columbia, one Teutprot, one Jewish, may exchange scholarly greetings at the corner of West 93rd Street and Broadway, under a notice in Spanish about the extermination of cockroaches (or *cucarachas*, which sounds sunnier), taking home German *bratwurst*, Greek *taramosalata*, Chinese beanshoots and perhaps a bottle of Chilean Burgundy from a Sicilian wine store. But the people of New York's varied communities are bound together by a force even more powerfully unifying than the appeal of the world's richest international cuisine. I mean their strong, shared, and for the most part healthy urge to make pots of money, which was why they came here and founded all these neighbourhoods in the first place.

The Neighbourhood Life of Harlem

PHOTOGRAPHS BY CHESTER HIGGINS

In "Strivers' Row", called that because the first blacks in the area had to work so hard to pay off huge mortgages, a proud young homeowner leaves for church.

The first blacks came to Harlem in the early 1900s in search of a better life. They willingly paid exorbitant rents to raise their children in what was then a spacious, clean new neighbourhood. The dream soured. Harlem became the most overcrowded area in the United States and a byword for decrepit housing, high unemployment and rampant crime. In spite of ample cause for despair, the hopes of many Harlem residents still burn high, fuelled by racial pride and some victories in their struggle to wrest control of their destinies from a political and economic system they feel has failed them. While working for improved housing, better schools and safer streets, they also preserve some old institutions—as sacred as churches, as prosaic as barbershops—that give this teeming city within a city a sense of community and, surprisingly, an almost small-town quality.

Tenants of small, stuffy rooms find fresh air and company on a doorstep.

For these friends a street provides as good a place to chat as a living room.

A woman gets a newspaper and "the buzz"—local gossip—from a newsvendor.

On a typical Harlem concourse, 119th St., new apartment blocks rise beyond old, shabby tenements adorned with fire escapes that are ugly but very necessary.

Their young spirits still a shield against the slum environment, boys join a friend on his way to a laundromat with a pillowcase full of his mother's washing.

Brimming with enthusiasm, Harlem children rally around their lively teacher. Throughout New York City, school windows are caged against persistent vandalism.

A young saleswoman orders merchandise by telephone for her shop, where black-consciousness-raising publications sell as steadily as fancy whisk brooms.

His oversized sunglasses and wide lapels conforming to fashions set by younger men, a proud driver shows off his new Cadillac, a tangible sign of his success.

A joke elicits a rollicking response from a youth.

A beaming woman barber banters with customers.

A fashionable lady in mink scarf rushes to church.

A smiling woman greets friends from her window.

Fresh fish, rare in this frozen-food era, give this street an old-time look.

On a street, a vegetable vendor competes with white-owned supermarkets.

To feast on dishes blacks knew in the southern U.S.—cornbread, hominy grits, collard greens—customers flock to Adelle's Kitchen, a popular eating place.

A man relaxes in a shop that has the air of a small-town general store.

Barbershops like this one—the Celebrity Unisex on Seventh Avenue—are traditional Harlem social centres, where friends exchange jokes, news and opinions.

4

Where the Money Is

Immigrants lining up on Ellis Island did not come to admire the scenery but to get in there and make a living. New York City is a place where the crafts of economic survival, competition, self-assertion are practised sedulously. It is a city crammed with money, the capital of the world's capital; and yet there is a strangely old-fashioned, small-town quality about much of its economic life.

We expect from a plutopolis a concentration of concerns, a handful of mighty corporations, giants that strive to be more gigantic still by eating other giants—and, indeed, we find them here. Almost a fifth of America's 500 biggest corporations have their headquarters in New York City (although the number, for reasons we shall come to, has been waning) and scores of large foreign companies run their U.S. or Western Hemisphere operations from here as well. From broadcasters to distillers to insurers and oil producers, corporate titans in every commercial field have engraved their names on the city's geography with their skyscrapers. RCA, McGraw Hill, Seagram, General Motors, Mobil, Pan Am, Woolworth, Lever, Chase Manhattan, Chrysler, Columbia Broadcasting System—a map of Manhattan reads like a directory of Big Business.

But the names of those skyscrapers, monstrous images of corporateness, frequently conceal a significant truth: that within them there are thousands and thousands of comparatively small enterprises. The tiny factories in downtown Manhattan, the narrow streets full of the ghosts of cart-horses, find counterparts galore in the tiny firms housed in the citadels of the giants—a couple of typewriters, a telephone, a little family of employees. Thirty workers is about the average for a city manufacturer, half that number for a city business. New York is a town of small capitalists —about a couple of hundred thousand—as well as big ones, and the diversity of their enterprises matches the mixed bundle of crafts and skills brought in by the immigrant ships.

Other cities grow wealthy through specialization. Detroit is powered by the internal combustion engine, as Chicago was once fed with butcher's meat. And yet specialization, although economically rewarding, can also be dangerous. When depression comes to an industry, as it does periodically to the motor industry, the specialist city suffers and has nowhere to turn. New York's strength has always lain in diversification. Moreover, the very ability to diversify, to adjust economically to changing situations, is taken to be a gloriously positive attribute of the city's temper, not just a rough necessity imposed by circumstances.

We see this in the rapidly changing fortunes of New York as a port. Shipping was once the city's primary reason for existence and the statistics are still impressive: the 23 miles of quays and moles; the 13 railways that trundle imports inland and bring cargo to be shipped abroad; the scooping up weekly of tons of rusted metal, boxes, bottles, dead cats and rats from the waters (as well as a modest dozen corpses every year). But New York City's greatest days as a port are done.

My last trips by sea—on the *Michelangelo* and *Rafaello* to and from Naples—will soon, in memory, become mixed up with movies from the 1930s, in which transatlantic travel was a whole culture. It is pretty well finished—the age of the million passengers a year being met by Checker cabs, and the fine human mess of the Customs inspection, from 44th to 57th Streets. A lot of the cargo shipping has moved to the New Jersey side of the Hudson, where container services have brought down the cost of loading and unloading. Besides the fact that crowded Manhattan docks lack the space for conversion to handling the large containers, port workers there have shown hearty dislike for the system. Shippers have shown an equal dislike for New York as a port because of its unreliable—or all too reliable—human element. It acquired a reputation for too much crime and corruption on the waterfront, too many wildcat strikes.

The Port of New York Authority says this image is dead and superseded by that of the city as a revitalized shipping centre. In any case, the decline in the industry was less disastrous than it might have been because New York, with characteristic adaptability and foresight, long ago took account of the fact that the Hudson had two banks, only one of which belonged to the city, and tied up its fate as a port with those of possible competitors. Established in 1921, the Port of New York Authority is responsible for all port installations within a 25-mile radius of the Statue of Liberty. Through this powerful and financially self-sufficient body, the fortunes of the whole area as a shipping centre are pooled. If the super-efficient container operation at Elizabeth, New Jersey, now handles much cargo that once would have gone through New York City, the city's maritime facilities, thanks to the Port Authority, are not impoverished. Thus Manhattan, even in an era of decreasing passenger traffic, can have, on the Hudson, between 48th and 52nd Streets, a modern, heated and air-conditioned passenger-ship terminal capable of accommodating six liners at once. And thus the Port of New York—admittedly an entity encompassing much more than just the port of New York City—can still proclaim itself the nation's busiest, handling more than 20 million tons of cargo a year.

The diverse nature of the Port Authority's responsibilities, which extend well inland, attest to New York's adaptability. Under its aegis towers the World Trade Center, two huge blocks and subsidiary buildings providing nine million square feet of office space in Manhattan's Lower West Side. The authority controls six of the main bridges and tunnels (which produce

Two well-to-do matrons parade their symbols of wealth—expensive mink coats—along a Manhattan Street. The city remains a magnet for super-achievers who drive hard for success. Once they have money, they and their families tend to accumulate and flaunt possessions as a way of announcing their newly gained status.

a staggering and steady income from tolls), the Port Authority Trans-Hudson railway (known to New Yorkers as PATH), which ties Manhattan to New Jersey, two heliports, two great bus terminals and four major airports (Kennedy, La Guardia, Newark and Teterboro). Air transport services have boomed while shipping has been declining in relative importance. Kennedy Airport's growth may be examined statistically with some profit—fewer than a quarter of a million passengers in 1949, when Kennedy was still Idlewild, nearly 20 million some 20 years later. Air freight went up a couple of hundredfold in that time.

Importing and exporting—people and goods—is big stuff. New York is more of a handler than a producer. Less than one quarter of its four million white-collar workers are employed by companies that actually make things. It is a town of services, trade, finance, insurance, real estate, transport, public utilities, with about a quarter of a million people collecting pay-checks from the municipality itself.

If New York can be said to have any manufacturing specialization it is to be found in the garment industry in mid-Manhattan, although most of the work is done in Brooklyn, Queens, the Bronx, the Lower East Side—work subcontracted to little firms in little factories. It is an industry that proclaims its immigrant origins—one suitable for cheap labour in airless sweatshops, with undernourished Jewish tailors staggering from street to street with sewing-machines on their backs. There are few consumptive seamstresses now in heavily unionized New York. Although some clothing firms are moving south, the industry still provides work for nearly a quarter of a million, and it is unlikely ever to be seriously depressed. People will always need to conceal, or wantonly half-reveal, their nudity in modest stylishness or face the sharp northern winter in furs. New York dressmaking serves this need. It deals in craft more than art and originates very little *haute couture*.

Only human fingers can create art, and New York's garment industry is a child of the machine—specifically the sewing-engine that Elias Howe fathered in 1846. We ought, for a moment, to take off our hats to Howe and feel vicariously guilty about his fate. America did not at first want his invention, so he sold patent rights in England for £250. Returning to America destitute, his wife dying, he found the country whirring with sewing machines—unauthorized copies of his patent, improved in design by another American inventor, Isaac Singer. Howe fought a battle in the courts and managed to re-establish his rights in 1854, and in the remaining dozen years of his life, received royalties. This is, I suppose, a kind of American success story.

The growth of the industry in New York owed more to immigrant German Jews than to home-fostered enterprise. Paris, home of *haute couture*, was never interested in an off-the-peg dress industry, but Germany, home of the military uniform, was exporting overcoats busily

On the Hudson River, just opposite Manhattan on the New Jersey side, derelict barges that once served busy New York harbour rot in the mud at their moorings.

in the 1870s, loose un-Prussian mantles made in Berlin by about 70 machine shops. When more than half a million Jews came over from Germany and its neighbours—Russia, Poland, Rumania, Austria—in the last decades of that century, they were ready to extend the ready-made principle to more delicate garments, and Howe's brain-child was there to show them how. The man or woman concerned with the hand-made, and able to afford it, still goes to Paris, Rome or London, but the rest of us are children of the child of the machine.

I might mention also that the American Civil War, which was good to New York—or rather to New York's financiers—in several ways gave the city's manufacturers an opportunity to work out new methods for the mass-production of uniforms. When peace came, all that the industry needed was a new breed of designers. The breed flourishes now, but the moguls of the trade are plagiarists of Paris. Go to Ohrbach's Oval Room on 34th Street, and you will find women lining up at seven in the morning to get the new Right Bank designs red-hot. There is no substitute for Parisian chic but there is little, to my eye, wrong with New York elegance. After all, the *haute couture* is always for the few, and Paris girls as a generality are neatly made but not outstanding in dress sense. As the advertisers put it, New York mini-salaried stenographers can look like a million dollars. They are well served by Saks and Altman and Bonwit Teller and Bergdorf Goodman and Bloomingdale's and Macy's and Gimbels and other department stores, to which they disburse something approaching a billion dollars annually.

New York's creative gifts are so richly devoted to selling that the city's wholesale trade accounts for about $80 billion a year, and its retail for about $13 billion. There is an art in selling, and it is seriously studied in Madison Avenue, which sells to the city, the nation and the world. By Madison Avenue, I mean the great advertising agencies, not the street itself, where, in fact, few of them make their homes these days. They are scattered through midtown Manhattan. In those agencies men and women of very considerable verbal and pictorial talent cultivate an economy of advertising style (in which wit and taste play their parts) that the world is almost prepared to accept as high art. The days of the brash, manic, over-persuasive technique are long gone, and sometimes the best parts of the magazines we buy are the advertisements. When, during the Second World War, special economy editions of *Life* were prepared for GIs overseas, containing news and articles but no advertisements, the troops rejected them as lacking an essential glamorous ingredient.

It may not be fanciful to look for the origins of Madison Avenue advertising style in New York Jewish speech—laconic, dry, a mix of Yiddish and English, irreverent, the very dialect of urban experience. *Nim a nosh a nickel* (Have a bite for five cents), which one used to see in delicatessens, may not be great art but it is highly economical persuasion.

Recently I saw an advertisement for Irish whisky that said: "Scotch is a fine beverage and deserves its popularity. But enough is enough already." Advertising language does not have to be Yiddish, but it has to avoid Teutprot rotundity. There just isn't space on the side of a bus for more than a curt epigram, nor the time on television for more than a few seconds of comic drama with a selling punch.

Manhattan is the headquarters of the major radio and television networks, and they are sustained by their commercial breaks. In terms of the art of broadcasting—as those of us brought up on the BBC know it—it is now gloomily accepted that America, shackled by obsessions with ratings, can never reach the heights. The best American television—with the exception of the news shows—is, alas, what is bought cheaply from Britain and presented on the public broadcasting channels. The commercial channels dare not present drama of such urgent import that the viewer chafes with impatience when the commercials cut in; at the same time they must not present the viewer with the ambiguities, longueurs and cerebration inseparable from great dramatic art, lest he lose patience and flick over to a less demanding channel.

A visitor to America like myself gets from the commercial networks what he cannot get in Europe—free entree to a museum of old movies and the pleasure of the commercials themselves. For the art of the television commercial—which is strongly influencing technique in the cinema—is a very considerable one, and its intrinsic virtues sometimes so great that one remembers the commercial and forgets what it is being commercial about. A man is shown waking dyspeptically in the night and saying: "I can't believe I ate the *whole* thing." This hits frightening depths in the mind, but it is hard to remember what he uses to relieve the indigestion.

Sometimes a rich sponsor will allow the transmission of a programme without commercial interruptions—some great piece of American cinematic art at a time of rejoicing, such as Thanksgiving or Easter. I thus remember seeing a Doris Day movie about junketings on table tops in Paris without the blessed relief of sharper and more literate cuttings-in of advertisements. Previously, though, we were shown the late Pasolini's *Gospel According to Saint Matthew*, rich with interludes of hard-selling. Christ's being nailed to the cross was interrupted by a rugged cowboy riding into the flaming sunset, his voice-over saying that now he had changed to some healthful product or other he was going to live forever. This seemed to me indiscreet.

The typewriter, like the sewing-machine, is one of Manhattan's major engines—a guillotine, however, more than an instrument for expansive lyricism. The advertising engineers labour at the ultimate economy of material in the city where Maxwell Perkins, king of literary editors, strove to sufflaminate the logorrhea of Thomas Wolfe, who was said to need a wheelbarrow to deliver the manuscripts of his novels. This is a place of

In Manhattan's garment district, a delivery man (right) leans against the weight of the trolley he is pulling and two others (above) take a break on a busy street. A 30-block area of workshops and factories, the garment district is only a part of the city's widespread apparel industry which employs some 200,000 workers.

editors more than creators. I, who call myself a sort of literary creator, know all too well the difficulty of writing a book in Manhattan. Life calls; the mere recording of life is for somewhere duller. Besides, one lives for the day in New York—it is presumptuous to think one may be alive tomorrow—and a book is more than a day's work.

But editing, clipping, carving and polishing are in order. New York, or the publishing district of midtown Manhattan, dressmakes typescripts for selling and may, with Boston as a lesser planet, be regarded as the English-speaking world's commercial publishing capital. I say "commercial" without disparagement. One does not bring a specialist study of Florentine incunabula or proto-Gallic surnames to a New York publishing house. One takes it to a university press in Princeton or Ann Arbor. Books in London publishing firms were, until recently, the sort of commodity a gentleman might promote in modest affluence or dignified poverty; in New York an author feels ashamed if he offers work that has no whiff of a bestseller.

Printing and publishing—of newspapers and magazines as well as block-buster novels—take care of about 120,000 of the city's workers and hence amount to a considerable industry. Following the dressmaking pattern, if New York sells clothes to itself with the manic energy with which it sells them to the nation, so it also goes in for bookselling on a scale undreamt of in other American cities. You will find comparatively few books on sale in Oklahoma City, but you will meet too many in New York. The selling of books is a cold-blooded craft, so that even remaindering—the selling of remaining stock at low prices, which in Europe is a sign of a book's failure—is a minor industry in itself. Book clubs, which proliferate here, handle much of the book glut nowadays. A book on sale in Brentano's at ten dollars can be bought for one dollar from a book club, functioning, if I may coin the term, as a remaindery.

New York's multiplicity and diversity of trades and commodities usually help it over the economic hurdles—except when, as with the Wall Street Crash of 1929, panic hits the flow of capital. In the 1970s a growing failure of prosperity began to promote fear which, in its turn, made recession deepen further. Manufacturing declined and this, along with an increase in mergers and automation, hurt the unskilled and semi-skilled—meaning mainly the so-called ethnic minorities. Firms began to leave the city and set up elsewhere for three compelling reasons: the growth of theft and violence, exorbitant rents and high city taxes.

When a company seeks to expand (and the alternative is always contraction) it must face the problem of a rent increase, and when rents account for more than a quarter of its outgoings, a site in New Jersey or Connecticut or upstate New York must seem more attractive. The city fathers, fearing the growing loss of tax-money, have tried to stem the exodus of business by buying waste land in Brooklyn, the Bronx, Queens and Staten Island and offering it to manufacturers at a rent lower than

Inured to the fortune in diamonds and gold spread before her in the shop window, a bored saleslady stands lost in thought during the slack late afternoon hour. The shop is one of many that cluster around 47th Street, Manhattan's "Diamond Row", where 80 per cent of all diamond trading in the United States is carried on.

anything private landlords would exact. They have even been adding the inducement of an option to buy. Still, the flight of business has continued. In the first half of the 1970s New York City lost half a million jobs.

When discussing any aspect of New York life we always revert, sooner or later, to the problem of violence. Businessmen are, at bottom, ordinary human beings who do not relish being mugged at the end of a hard day. Warehouses and offices are too frequently burgled and the cost of security —guards, alarms, complex locks—steadily grows. Trucks carrying freight are hijacked so often that some move through the city streets in convoys protected by armed guards. Then there are the taxes, which the business-man sees as mostly going to the support of people who do not wish to work. It is true that public assistance for the unemployed and unemployable accounts for a great chunk of city tax, so the problem feeds on itself: the more unemployed, the higher the taxes; the higher the taxes, the more businesses leave town; the more businesses leave town, the more un-employed. In 1976 about one in eight New Yorkers was on welfare, and the ratio was growing.

The failure of trade is especially sad in the context of a community uniquely equipped for prosperty. All the talent of the world is here, along with masses of skilled labour. Moreover, there is a capacity for coping with sudden change, for grasping new techniques, for dealing with highly imaginative projects that would daunt the citizens of lesser cities.

And yet New York, like Great Britain, knows the meaning of the term "brain drain". Brilliant young men are leaving, and other brilliant young men are refusing to come in. The lure of corporate ambition and culture and entertainment and civic beauty is not as strong as once it was.

On the other hand, the dream of finding a better life—for soul, body and business—in the suburbs or in other American cities is often revealed as no more than a dream. There is plenty of theft and violence everywhere, and a body called the Association for a Better New York has been asking businessmen to swallow a swift, very dry Martini and take a long, sober look at the facts.

Mugging, thieving and hijacking were not invented in New York; if there seem to be more of these commodities in New York than elsewhere —well, New York is bigger than elsewhere. Anyway, they are inescapable aspects of modern living. As for office rents, they may be high in New York but they are hardly low in St. Louis and Atlanta. Do not long for escape to peaceful California; see how the Californians are coming to New York. A failure of confidence is a subjective phenomenon and needs to be countered with tough bouts of positive thinking. This is Fun City, the ultimate fruit of Civilization, the place where the Corporate Action is, the Big Apple. And so on and so on. Many remain unconvinced. Even the New York Stock Exchange, sick of being singled out for special taxes, has talked of moving to New Jersey. We have already glanced at Wall Street. Let us take a closer look.

There used to be a wall here—a palisade of wood that stretched from the Hudson to the East River, designed to keep the Indians out. A thousand or so people lived in its shelter when it was the core of New Amsterdam, comforted also by a strong fort built to the south. A windmill and a canal —the "Ditch"—gave the tiny settlement a true Dutch look, although Indian canoes wove in and out among the merchantmen lying at anchor on the East River, into which the Ditch debouched. A ferry plied between New Amsterdam and Long Island. It was a wooden city and much plagued by fires, and Governor Peter Stuyvesant, banging out an order with his wooden leg, insisted on brick. Wooden pavings gave place to stone, beginning with a street called, appropriately, Stone Street. As for Stuyvesant's wooden wall to keep out the Indians, this was more symbolic than genuinely defensive: the citizens liked to rip out chunks for firewood or for their house-walls. In 1699 the English settlers pulled it down and called the blank space a street.

It was not until nearly a century later that two dozen traders, in the shade of that buttonwood tree that still flourishes in the soil of Wall Street myth (a plane tree, if anyone is interested, bearing knobs like buttons), made a pact about fair trading and set up rules concerning securities. They were dealing with the problems involved in the issue by the 1789-90 Congress of $80-million worth of stock to help pay the costs of the Revolutionary War. Investors were not willing to buy stock if they had no assurance they could also sell it. Hence the birth of a free and open market for the two-way passage of securities.

Following the British example—it was how Lloyd's, the great marine insurers, began—they made their centre of operations a coffee-house, the Tontine, of which only the old sign is left. Wall Street was an unremarkable home of finance until the Civil War, which was substantially underwritten by New York financiers.

There are rich names in this part of Manhattan—John Pierpont Morgan, Sr., James Stillman, George F. Baker—and the names bind together, in the utmost sincerity, money and sanctimony. John Pierpont Morgan, Sr., wrote in his will: "I commit my soul into the hands of my Savior, in full confidence that having redeemed it and washed it in His most precious blood, He will present it faultless before my Heavenly Father, and I intreat my children to maintain and defend at all hazard and at any cost of personal sacrifice the blessed doctrine of complete atonement for sin through the blood of Jesus Christ once offered and through that alone." And when he died in Rome in 1913, he committed to his son, John Pierpont Morgan, Jr., new head of the House of Morgan, the control of the Morgan interests in New York: four national banks, three trust companies, three life insurance companies, ten railroad systems, three street railway companies, an express company, and a shipping trust. To quote the American novelist

John Dos Passos, an acute observer of his country's social scene, "the interwoven cables of the Morgan Stillman Baker combination held credit up like a suspension bridge, thirteen percent of the banking resources of the world". During the great steel strike of 1919, J. P. Morgan, Jr. stood out for the open shop: "I believe American principles of liberty are deeply involved, and must win if we stand firm."

Money, faith, idealism—these go together and conjoin with war. The banks of New York, it is said, were responsible for saving the Union. When the Union troops were trounced at Bull Run, Lincoln turned naturally to a group of New York bankers. Moses Taylor—head of City Bank of New York and treasurer of the New York, Newfoundland and London Telephone Company—pledged $750 million in gold and helped win the war. He thereby assured himself of an admirer's accolade as a "competent executive and an ardent patriot", in that order.

The opening up of the West, the war with Spain, the Liberty Loans of the First World War—these helped the growth of New York banking substantially to say the least. The power of the banks today is reflected in the architectural magnificence of the Wall Street district. This is the most patriotic part of New York and perhaps the most pious.

Money is money, small sums add up to big ones, the daily work of New York wrings dollars out of everything—diamonds at Tiffany's, frozen custard, the transportation of harps, chiromancy, Oedipus complexes, mugging, business-is-lousy cigar bargains, imitation faeces, colas and uncolas, geriatry, pediatrics, striptease, automobile accessories, Belgian waffles, loans, the calling in of loans, real estate, unreal estate, everything. The stress of Manhattan industriousness is best seen when the day's work is over and the transport systems are crammed. The barbarous bad temper is a great wonder. Then the lights come on and Manhattan prepares for the evening. The evening is another day.

The Big Parade

PHOTOGRAPHS BY DAN BUDNIK

Behind policemen sheltering as they wait for the parade to begin, giant balloons of cartoon characters are tethered with nets to keep them from floating away.

Down New York's wide avenues, more than a dozen parades a year make their exuberant way. One of the best loved of all is the Thanksgiving Day procession staged by Macy's department store each autumn. First held in 1924, it has become a New York tradition. Not even rain, as the following pages happily prove, can keep at home the thousands who turn out to watch it, or dampen the spirits of the participants, many of them Macy's volunteers, who assemble as early as dawn. At 9.30 a.m. the amazing cavalcade of marching bands, mammoth balloons (some five storeys tall) and brilliant floats moves off on its two-mile-long route. For three hours its colour, dash and gaiety are an antidote to the November chill; then, with the last float gone, the crowds disperse, the streets revert to traffic and New York heads into the grey gloom of winter.

Weighted down with crimson sandbags, a popular children's TV character heads a row of helium-filled balloons waiting in a side street to join the procession.

A rain-soaked crew of volunteers manhandles the limp bulk of Raggedy Andy, one of America's best-loved story-book characters, towards its place on a float.

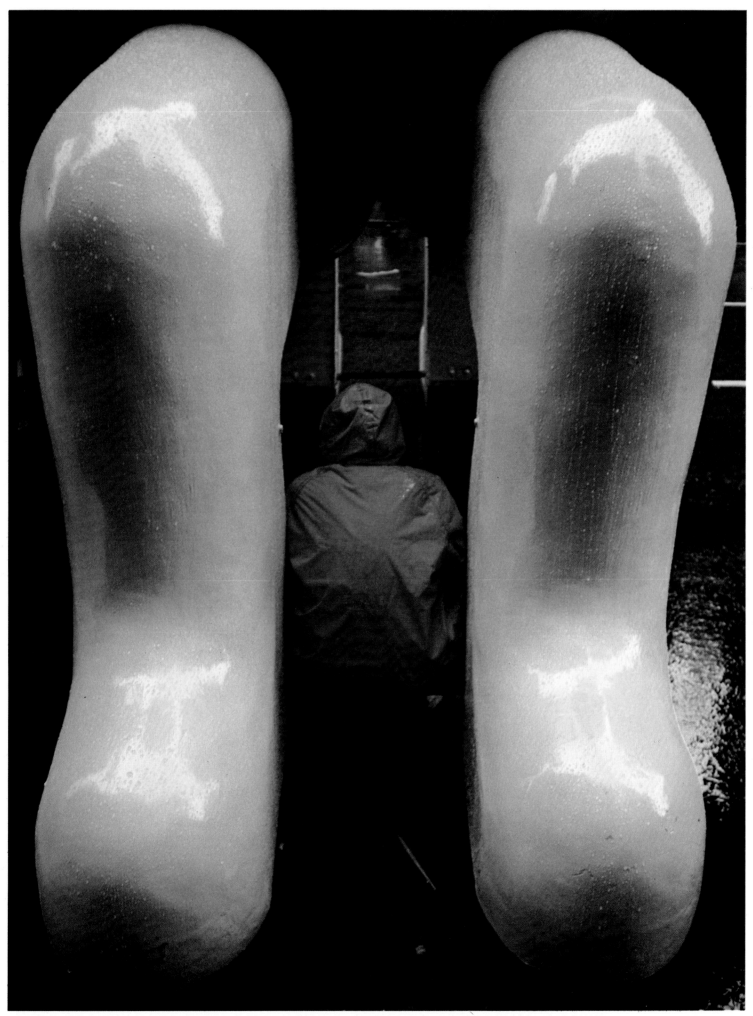

His preparations completed, a helper huddles for shelter between the gleaming hindlegs of an 18-foot-high fantasy bug, modelled on a familiar children's toy.

Children gathered at an apartment window along the route wait excitedly for the parade's arrival.

A raincoated family on a fire escape cranes for a first view.

In the glistening street a military-style band passes in perfect formation. Even when weather reduces the crowds there may be half a million spectators.

Accompanying the Wizard of Oz float, the Tin Man waves to the crowd, undaunted by his sodden silver suit.

Dressed as a gilded pineapple and draped with the same fruit, an indomitable young marcher reinforces the parade's carnival note with her flashing smile.

A national fire-prevention symbol, Smokey the Bear moves proudly along Central Park West.

Smokey arrives at the parade's end outside Macy's entrance (right), only to capsize ignominiously as strong winds finally defeat his crew of weary handlers.

5

The Great White Way

In the evening Broadway becomes the Great White Way and Manhattan is manifestly the entertainment capital of the world. I can claim to have known two aspects of New York life from the inside—academia and the musical theatre. I can, indeed, claim—and I doubt if this would be possible in any other city of the world—to have known them at the same time. Some years ago I was a Distinguished Professor at City College, lecturing on James Joyce and Shakespeare and then catching aeroplanes to Minneapolis or Toronto or Boston, to tinker with the book and lyrics I had written for a musical adaptation of *Cyrano de Bergerac.*

Soon it was not a matter of catching aeroplanes but of riding the subway. *Cyrano*, after its provincial try-outs, was on Broadway. My name was not up in lights but it was printed large on the posters outside the Palace Theater I had achieved a mythical ambition. To arrive on Broadway—meaning some playhouse or other in the region around Times Square—is the dream of everybody whose life is, wholly or partly, in thrall to the stage. London's Shaftesbury Avenue has not one-tenth of Broadway's glamour, and this is probably unjust. But theatre and justice have little to do with each other (or so I felt, anyway, when *Cyrano* closed after only 49 performances).

At the start of this century the flavour of Broadway was hardly distinguishable from that of Shaftesbury Avenue, and even musical comedy, which was to become Broadway's supremely original contribution to world theatre, was a pale imitation of what Europe could offer. New York had not been able to match the Gilbert and Sullivan it had so shamelessly pirated (as many as eight theatres putting on unauthorized versions of *Patience* or *Pinafore*), and the pretty confections of Rudolph Friml and Victor Herbert were European operetta *Schaumwein* allowed to go flat.

George M. Cohan, the Irishman whose statue stands in Times Square, was a great American versatile—actor, playwright, composer, singer, dancer. He was also one of the first to recognize that musical entertainment did not have to be sealed off from the real world in a highly adorned but airtight vacuum. "The Broadway man," he observed, "has a better idea of life and things in general than any other class of man in the world. He sees more, meets more and absorbs more in a day than the average individual will in a month."

Cohan's own songs—*Yankee Doodle Dandy, Mary, Nelly Kelly, Over There, Give my Regards to Broadway*—were themselves a mixture of brashness and sentimentality, but they were also pioneer examples of an art that was to start flowering after the First World War.

Lit by a jumble of neon signs, a restless surge of people throngs the sidewalk along 42nd Street, just off Times Square, as though it were still midday. But the clock projecting from the wall registers the real time—12.30 a.m.

Meanwhile, the theatre-going public wanted trombones, red noses and ankles. Florenz Ziegfeld gave Broadway his own unique style of girl-show with his *Ziegfeld Follies*. Decking (if that is the right word) his chorines in daring, knee-length bathing suits, he set about "Glorifying the American Girl". Will Rogers, a comic star of the *Follies*, said: "Ziegfeld took Michelangelo's statues, took some fat off them with a diet of lamb chops and pineapples, then he . . . brought the statues to life, only with better figures, and the only marble about them was from the ears north."

Faced with this kind of competition, the serious theatre made little headway. The New Theater, formed with its own resident company in 1909, and more concerned with art than bumper box-office returns, collapsed after only two seasons. Even by 1916 there were only three serious dramas amongst the welter of musical comedies, farces and revues. But the new and adventurous techniques of Dublin's Abbey Theatre, which first visited New York in 1911, and the productions of the Vieux-Columbier company, which came over from Paris in 1917, scattered seeds that were to germinate and produce fine fruit.

The Provincetown Players, formed to encourage original works by American dramatists, made their first appearance in New York in 1916. Eugene O'Neill was nurtured in the group and gave America its first play to win a serious international reputation—*Beyond the Horizon*—in 1920. The Theater Guild, started in 1919 on a seasonal subscription basis, was not only adventurous in the European way but also commercially successful. By its fourth season the Guild had 12,000 subscribers and in 1925 it opened its own million-dollar theatre on 52nd Street. It was this early post-war period that saw Robert Sherwood's urbane and witty *Road to Rome* and Laurence Stallings' and Maxwell Anderson's anti-war comedy, *What Price Glory?* Elmer Rice, in *The Adding Machine*, dramatized the dehumanization of the white-collar worker and beat the Expressionists of Germany at their own game in a work that is essentially American.

Visiting New York in 1923, the Moscow Art Theatre Company was impressed by the ensemble playing it saw and began to teach the now-famous "method" devised by Konstantin Stanislavsky, in which the actor strives for total involvement in the character he portrays.

Broadway was growing up. Broadway was becoming itself. Although Hollywood had already begun its long infancy and the theatre had to fight against moving shadows, the number of Broadway productions almost doubled in seven years, from 150 in the 1920-21 season to 280 in 1927-28. Broadway, being American, has always set great store by quantity.

But the Wall Street crash of 1929, coinciding with the birth of talking pictures, permanently blighted Broadway's prosperity. The annual number of productions dropped drastically and since then has never risen to more than about 70—still, of course, a remarkable figure compared with the rest of the world, not excepting London. There was no call to construct new and

Wherever pedestrian traffic is heavy in New York, there invariably are street vendors who hawk food to hungry passers-by from carts. This one—who offers ices, as well as plump, salted pretzels the year round—finds a busy trade in night-time Times Square.

opulent theatres; expansion rather took the form of an incredible growth of new talent. Playwrights such as Clifford Odets, Sidney Kingsley, Lillian Hellman, Thornton Wilder and William Saroyan began to incorporate that element of social protest in their work that has, ever since the 1930s, been an almost essential ingredient of serious drama. The post-war period has seen Tennesee Williams, Arthur Miller, William Inge and Edward Albee.

As for collective enterprises, the Group Theater, with its devotion to Stanislavsky's ideals, kept going. From 1947, however, it was the Actors' Studio that most thoroughly cultivated the "method" and produced not only new stage actors but also a new breed of screen actors. The permanent company that Orson Welles and John Houseman maintained at the Mercury Theater just before the Second World War also gained international prestige in 1941 with the film *Citizen Kane*, which gave Welles's originality of approach and the ensemble strength of his actors the advantage of cinematic fluidity.

In spite of this record, however, New York is not pre-eminent in "straight" dramatic enterprises. Broadway playwrights have their own originality but, except for Eugene O'Neill, they have never fired the world of theatre with new approaches comparable with the Brecht revolution in Germany or the Absurdist movement in France. Moreover, by the mid-1970s New York managements were depending very heavily on British importations of straight drama.

The city also lacks a tradition of classical theatre. It has no Shakespearian tradition, unless the jazzed-up, deliberately "popular" open-air enterprises staged in Central Park each summer by Joseph Papp may be taken as a legitimate mode of Shakespeare presentation. Papp succeeds by approaching the technique of the Broadway musical—a field in which no American need fear competition.

For Broadway is the originator of a form of musical entertainment that is brilliantly and inimitably its own, powered by a dynamic not to be found in the Old World, nor for that matter—except for this incredible enclave— very much in the New. Since New York is a kind of vertical Europe with a dollop of Africa, the originality of the Broadway musical must have its roots in something European, with a tinge of something darker. Jazz had already begun to enthral the American public, when, in 1921, an all-Negro musical show called *Shuffle Along* was presented on Broadway. The show was a smash hit and was followed within a period of four years by eight similar shows, including *Liza*, *Runnin' Wild* and *Chocolate Dandies*. As the show-business newspaper *Variety* reported, this black entertainment combined "pep, pulchritude, punch and presentation".

We must probably look to the New York Jew for the urban sophistication that came to distinguish so many subsequent Broadway musicals. American Jews who have made good have done so very frequently through the Arts, both fine and demotic. They have been impresarios and heads of film studios; but they have also been creators and performers. The tradition of New York comedy—the broad, popular structure on which the Broadway musical is laid—derives from burlesque and vaudeville, and the staple idiom of that tradition comes, it seems, in part from what Yiddish has done to English. The tongue I like to call Yidglish is a medium implicit with the tragi-comedy of the urban experience. It is already the stuff of art in its concern with economy of expression and its reliance not on vocabulary but on inversion and stress.

The following typically New York Yidglish expressions are natural stage material: Get lost; You should live so long; I need it like a hole in the head; Alright already (this became the refrain of a song in *Guys and Dolls*); From that he makes a *living*?; Go hit your head against the wall; *This* I need yet?; You want it should sing, too?; With sense, he's loaded; I should have such luck; On him it looks good.

I have taken this catalogue from Leo Rosten's *The Joys of Yiddish*. I take also from him a number of categories of ways in which English may be modified in the direction of the serio-comic:

Dismissal via *shm*-reduplication: "Fat-shmat, so long as she's happy." My favourite in this category comes from academia. I heard one Harvard professor say to another: "To hell with your theory. I've got data." The reply was: "Data-shmata—I *like* my theory." Emphasis through inverted word-order: "My son-in-law he wants to be." Fearful curses sanctioned by nominal cancellation: "A fire should burn in his heart, God forbid." Derision through interrogation: "I should pay him for such devoted service?" As for Yiddish loan-words, there are enough even in the language of British show-business to indicate where the power lies. In both Shaftesbury Avenue and the BBC Television Centre I have heard terms like *schmaltz, megillah, schmuck, schtik*, from impeccably Anglo-Saxon lips.

It is not perhaps too fanciful to look for a more generalized Jewish sound in that fusion of jazz and drawing-room ballad that is the American (really New York) popular song. The cult of mother, for instance, apotheothized in Al Jolson's *Mammy*, achieves a sentimental fullness of expression that true Teutprot sensibilities find antipathetic. It was sung by a New York Jew in blackface who alleged that this mammy came from Alabama (the only available rhyme except for "hammy" and "clammy"), and here we have the typical conflation of Jew and Negro in an expression of exilic longing. To both Jewish immigrants and black slaves, home is across the Jordan. Songs about wishing to be back in California, Carolina, Texas, or any other state of the Union, are general cries of exile given a local habitation.

Perky songs about attractive girls, like the *If You Knew Susie* that Eddie Cantor sang, seem to be the wish-fulfilments of New York Jews wanting easy relationships—usually with easy-going Teutprot women—which the traditional ethic forbade. Where the songs are emotional, they drip—even

A landmark in itself, Times Square has landmarks of its own to offer visitors who come to stare at its dazzling lights. Among them is the 58-foot-tall cigarette billboard (above). Out of the smoker's open mouth comes a steady stream of oversize smoke rings that are in fact nothing more than harmless steam.

in their harmonies—with a Central European soulfulness. The saxophone, a very gentile instrument used in the Paris production of Wagner's *Tannhäuser* in the 1860s, lent itself to the throbbings of sentimental frustration. Before the Broadway musical could properly develop, the Tin Pan Alley sound had to be in full flesh.

Tin Pan Alley was the midtown Manhattan region of the popular music companies—Leo Feist, Remick, Mills and Witmark, Shapiro-Bernstein. Song-writing as a mainly, although by no means exclusively, Jewish trade began here before the First World War. Irving Berlin's *Alexander's Ragtime Band*, for example, goes back to 1911. It was a song by a Jew about a black combo ("It's just de bestest band dat am, honeylamb.").

An area of eight blocks or so of cheap lodgings, bars and pool rooms, Tin Pan Alley was where song-writers tried to become Irving Berlins. There were George Meyer, who wrote *Me and My Gal*, Ernest Breuer, Lou Handman, Con Conrad (*Down in Dear Old New Orleans*), Irving Bibo, Joe Meyer (*Clap Hands, Here Comes Charlie*), Al Dubin, Dave Dreyer (*Me and My Shadow*). Although the selling of sheet music was a considerable industry—there was always someone in the family who could play the piano—songs were written for singers like Eddie Cantor, George Jessel, Al Jolson, for inclusion in shows like *Ziegfeld Follies*. The song-writers' aim was not to reach the parlour public direct, but through Broadway.

Conventions of form and content unite the worse excretions of Tin Pan Alley and the higher flights of Cole Porter or Rodgers and Hart, but the Broadway stage at its musical best belongs to a different planet from the one where *Barney Google* and *Does the Spearmint Lose its Flavor on the Bedpost Over Night?* make us bow our heads in shame.

The first great Broadway musical was *Show Boat*, as fresh now as it was in 1927, the music by Jerome Kern (with P. G. Wodehouse among the lyricists), the story taken from a successful novel by Edna Ferber. Here, perhaps inevitably, the most memorable song—*Ol' Man River*, sung by Paul Robeson—was one about the tribulations of the blacks, a cathartic for all the immigrant oppressed and their Teutprot oppressors alike.

The work as a whole had a lesson to teach that was not fully heeded until the 1940s: that the story of a musical should, if possible, be derived from a narrative structure (play or novel) powerful enough to stand on its own feet without the aid of song and dance. Cole Porter and the Gershwins too often wrote fine songs for musicals too weak to survive as drama.

Ira and George Gershwin raised the form to the level of genuine popular opera in 1935 with *Porgy and Bess*. Here was a story about blacks whose words and music were supplied by New York Jews. George Gershwin was a composer of large range, whose independent orchestral works use what is ultimately Tin Pan Alley material for a quasi-symphonic purpose. His *An American in Paris*, a kind of tone poem, was used for a ballet sequence in

Crowds flow out of a Broadway theatre after the curtain, many of them hastening to a late supper in one of the innumerable restaurants in all price ranges that cluster around New York's world-renowned entertainment district. The Booth (above), on the corner of 45th Street and Shubert Alley, is one of 30 or more theatres in the vicinity of Times Square.

a film musical of the same name and served a refinement, wit, sophistication previously unequalled but always, and still, implicit in the American musical comedy form.

Lorenz Hart and Richard Rodgers were luckier than most Broadway collaborators in that they worked with libretti (or "books") of solid dramatic worth and sometimes wit. Their Broadway partnership began in 1925 with *The Garrick Gaieties*, of which two songs became immortal: *Manhattan* and *Mountain Greenery*. Rodgers, in *On Your Toes* in 1936, introduced a jazz ballet, *Slaughter on Tenth Avenue*, which was choreographed by George Balanchine and established the principle that the dance element in a stage musical should be more than casual tap or mechanical high-kicking. The 1938 musical, *The Boys from Syracuse*, has the distinction of being better than Shakespeare's *The Comedy of Errors*, from which it is derived. *Pal Joey*, based on stories by John O'Hara and successfully produced in 1940, was so far ahead of its time in its serious realism that it had to wait until it was revived in 1952 to win the critical acclaim it deserved. It contained *Bewitched, Bothered and Bewildered*.

Hart died in 1943. The previous year Rodgers had already begun working with Oscar Hammerstein II on *Oklahoma!* Based on Lynn Riggs's play, *Green Grow the Lilacs*, the show opened on Broadway in 1943, where it had a run of 2,248 performances, went on to win a Pulitzer Prize and fixed for ever the principle that the book of a musical should be literate and even derive from a work of literature. Hammerstein's lyrics could never hope to compare with Hart's, but the Rodgers-Hammerstein combination is generally regarded as the main post-war glory of the New York stage.

The partnership produced such triumphs as *Carousel, South Pacific, The King and I, Flower Drum Song* (in which a San Franciscan Chinese girl begins a song in Yidglish: "I'm a girl and by me that's only great") and the huge, sentimental money-spinner *The Sound of Music*. This was "realistic" enough to have the Nazi regime in it and to have dealt with an authentic family, the von Trapps.

Encouraged by the commercial possibilities of musical adaptations of genuine literature, Alan Jay Lerner and Frederick Loewe in 1956 turned Bernard Shaw's *Pygmalion* into *My Fair Lady*, although, scared perhaps of being too literary, they made Professor Higgins split infinitives and burdened him with other grammatical solecisms. Still, anything seemed possible now. In the 1970s there was a musical based on Henry James's *The Ambassadors* (a flop), attempts at re-telling French history (*Pippin* and *Good Time Charlie*), a highly successful adaptation of Christopher Isherwood's *Goodbye to Berlin* called *Cabaret* and, with Stephen Sondheim's brilliant *A Little Night Music*, the stage adaptation of an Ingmar Bergman film. Edmond Rostand, the great French dramatist of the late 19th and early 20th Centuries, had been musicalized in *The Fantasticks*, and I was encouraged to follow this with, in *Cyrano*, more Rostand.

I have mentioned briefly musicals that depend on collective rather than individual talent, but I must not omit to point out that a good deal of Broadway's glory derives from great performers. Our own age has seen— indeed, in the single year 1964—three musicals that were essentially vehicles for stars. These were *Hello Dolly!*, with Carol Channing; *Funny Girl*, for Barbra Streisand and based on the life of Fanny Brice, herself one of the great Jewish comediennes; and *Fiddler on the Roof*, with Zero Mostel. The success of this last points again to the eminent suitability of Jewish tragi-comedy and, of course, high-flavoured Yidglish to the musical stage. The greatest Jewish performer of all, Al Jolson, overflowed the limits set by director and librettist and still personifies American Jewish dynamism, pure, raw Broadway.

Writing of Broadway, I am haunted by one Jewish figure who stands less for artistic talent than for the drive that enabled such talent to see the light. I mean Billy Rose, a Lower East Side Jew who began as a high-speed short-hand writer, tried to break into Tin Pan Alley as a song-writer but succeeded there only as a fighter for the song-writers' rights, became a night-club manager and a theatre-owner and ended, in my view, as the ultimate symbol, both fascinating and repulsive, of what Broadway is all about. He is also a symbol of a kind of elan hardly known in the Old World but frequently bred out of Jewish poverty and ambition in the New. The Yiddish word, *chutzpah*, expresses the imperturbable resilience, even cheekiness or gall, of the ghetto Jew. The *chutzpah* of the uneducated immigrant Jew was, in a sense, directed against Teutprot hegemony, and his ambition found one of the few outlets available to it through show-business.

Although Billy Rose was married for a time to Fanny Brice, he hankered after big, blonde gentile girls—the kind glorified by Ziegfeld. Rose imposed on Teutprot dignity the vital vulgarity that is at the bottom of even the most refined Broadway production. He did this when in 1937 he virtually took over the plans for the New York World's Fair. The organizers wanted a scholarly scenario dealing with American history. It was going to be correct, dignified and, by Broadway standards, ineffably dull.

Billy Rose said: "You want to make money, don't you?" People, he told them, wanted hot-dogs, colour, music, noise, nudity, spectacle, not Columbus making landfall and Washington crossing the Delaware. He sold his ideas to the organizers in a seance of vital, vulgar display, shouting, playing old American tunes on the harmonica, and the Fair Corporation signed him to put on a patriotic pageant in Flushing Meadows.

Rose ignored Washington, Hamilton and Jackson, and instead planned an "aquacade"— a water show with gorgeous girls, Johnny Weismuller (the original Tarzan), and Eleanor Holm, the Teutprot swimming champion Rose wished to marry. He brutally overrode the unions ("Don't worry about unions. Nobody who works for me ever has to join a union") and half-killed his performers. He planned four shows a day for seven days a week for two

Unmindful of cramped seating and cigarette smoke, jazz devotees listen transfixed as a fluegelhorn player blows a solo at the Village Vanguard jazz club in Greenwich Village. In clubs like this the mixing of ethnic artistic impulses—long a generating force in the city's musical creativity—continues.

years, and, in 1939, having watched President Roosevelt open the Fair and heard Albert Einstein speak of the wonders of science, he saw 8,500 people file in to see his aquacade.

The fair also offered 24 miles of soberer exhibits, including a parade of American accomplishments in the Court of Peace that had cost the United States $3.5 million. But the monumentally vulgar aquacade, with its purple water, flashing lights, comics, singers and near-naked beauties, pulled the public in. "It was a great hit," said one of the fair's chief planners, New York Parks Commissioner Robert Moses, "made Billy a lot of money and added to the public stock of harmless pleasure if not to the appreciation of American history." It was Broadway at its most self-assertive, Broadway triumphant. Among Billy Rose's other achievements was the authorship of the lyrics of *Barney Google* and *Does the Spearmint Lose its Flavor* on *the Bedpost Over Night?*

Billy Rose could hardly function on today's Broadway, with unions rather than great, greedy mavericks in charge of the theatrical profession. If anything is likely to kill Broadway, it is possibly the principles of unionism applied to an industry made for individualism or a collectivism unsubmissive to rules. When orchestral musicians demand feather-bedding (*viz.*, being paid for not performing in a minimum pit-band of 26 when the score itself may call for as few as ten players), seat-prices go up or productions faced with impossible budgets never get off the ground. Broadway has already ceased to be what it was. In the early 1970s there were only 35 major theatres left in the Times Square area. The cost of a theatrical night out—with taxis, dinner, drinks, modest seats in the stalls—could amount to a week's wages. Rowdyism and physical danger on the Great White Way was also another reason for staying at home and watching television.

For all that, it would be premature to say that the New York theatre is dying. In old commercial premises, restaurants, cellars, garages, churches, a modest form of drama flourishes: actors and technicians here find room denied them by the contraction of Broadway. There is now a vital Off-Broadway tradition, and an even livelier one Off-Off-Broadway. Blacks now form their own theatrical companies, so do Puerto Ricans. If the standards of dramaturgy and direction are comparatively low, at least theatre is fulfilling its ancient purpose of ritualizing life and providing a platform for voices that think they have something to say and often, in fact, really have.

The City Fathers are aware of the importance of theatre, in terms of amenity, commerce, even art. In 1972 building ordinances were revised to allow builders a bonus in floor space if they included a theatre in their structures. This enabled four new theatres to come into being in Times Square. It is a novel experience to get into a skyscraper elevator as though one were going to see one's psychiatrist and, instead and much more therapeutic, to be going to the theatre.

The city is also giving money to the drama and its sister arts, ballet and opera, either by direct grant or through peppercorn rents. Thus, the city bought an old library and allowed five little playhouses to be made out of it, charging the users one dollar a year. The same rent is attached to the City Center, formerly a vast Masonic temple, whose tax-free status additionally keeps the costs down, enabling the ballet and drama companies that perform there to charge only nominal admission prices. The city and the State of New York between them traditionally devote millions of dollars a year to the performing arts—either quixotic or shrewd, according to one's views of officialdom and art, but still a notable slice when one takes into account more urgent financial pressures.

The Lincoln Center for the Performing Arts is a superb example of what a city can do. In six buildings set around a waterscape one finds in residence the Metropolitan Opera, the New York City Opera, the New York Philharmonic, the New York City Ballet, a theatre company, an arts library and the Juillard School, that teaches music and dance. The Center draws something like three and a half million people every year.

The promotion of the performing arts in New York rests on a firm but modest foundation of local talent. In the New York manner, this talent is versatile, untemperamental, highly professional. The *répétiteur* of my own *Cyrano* left the show to become a conductor of Mahler in Milwaukee. Stanley Silverman plays guitar or banjo in a Broadway pit orchestra and then goes to a rehearsal of his new oratorio under Pierre Boulez. For Composer's Showcase performances in the Whitney Museum, singers and instrumentalists assemble from nowhere, do a single rehearsal of a work of hair-raising difficulty, then give a faultless public rendering without expectation of glowing critical praise. This professionalism, although it takes a very different form, is clearly of the same order as that which powered the flamboyant figures of the old Great White Way.

I admire the multiplicity of New York's artistic enterprises, as well as the invariably high standards of execution, but I do not come to Manhattan to see what I can see as well in London or Paris or Milan. For me, the uniqueness of what the city can offer resides in what an alchemy of cultures can do. The *temperamentvoll* East European Jews who tempered the tepid Englishry of my own city, Manchester, and turned it into the greatest musical centre of England, have also turned Teutprot New York into a place of dialectic, declamation, wry humour and song. This voluble and sensitive people, whose whole history is an epic of violence and passion, meets, through the medium of art, another enslaved race that remembers the intonations and rhythms of the African West Coast. Add the Celt, and you have an incredible mixture.

The artistic tradition that nurtured me was much concerned with understatement—admirable for drawing-room comedy but not the stuff of the great, bouncing Broadway stage. It is precisely the physical ebullience of the Broadway musical, combined with an urban wryness, that excites this foreigner. Two New York Jews—Leonard Bernstein and Stephen Sondheim—combine to remake *Romeo and Juliet* into *West Side Story*, a musical about West Side Teutprot-Puerto Rican conflict, adapting the tonalities of Stravinsky into a ballet that stuns with its energy, and a London critic exclaims: "These New Yorkers seem to be made of different blood and bone from ourselves." True. The Old World cannot match the ferocity of New York's popular art. Another Jew, Stephen Schwartz, sets the story of Jesus Christ in *Godspell*, and what would be an embarrassing collocation of pop-song and pseudo-religion from a British writer here works—drawing strength from the very unashamed vulgarity of the concept.

Broadway takes a story from Asia or Europe and, no matter how impeccable the simulation of local sound and colour, the Manhattan voice cuts in. Dolores Gray in *Kismet* sings of Baghdad, saying there has been nothing like it since Nineveh, adding, "Not since Babylon's hanging gardens went to pot, not since the day Gomorrah got too hot for Lot", and those un-rounded "-ot" rhymes strike a British ear with the very essence of the New York stage. *My Fair Lady* essays an exact reproduction of London in 1912 and ends up with rhymes like "bother me/rather be": New York endearingly breaks in. *The King and I* tries to implant New York neighbourliness in the palace of an Eastern despot, to the horror of that despot's real-life descendants. Bernstein and his collaborators try to put the Voltairian philosophy on the stage in *Candide* and present a bouncing, whirling musical that only Manhattan could have contrived.

Behind these immense and brilliant essays in energy, scented with sophistication that breaks into brashness, lies a New York tradition as old as the Jewish comedian, the bump and grind, the soft-shoe shuffle. The desperate dynamism is in the city itself. William Blake said "Energy is eternal delight", and he found that energy in hell.

6

How Things Work

It is characteristic of Broadway that it should make a musical about one of its mayors, the tubby, flamboyant Fiorello Henry La Guardia. And it is characteristic of New York that its political history should be so readily adaptable to dramatic (or musical) entertainment. Each decade has provided its own all-star bill of vaudeville heroes and villains, and the organization known as Tammany Hall was not only the richest repository of political power in New York (and often far beyond) but also the most exotic as well as the longest-running show in town.

Although Tammany Hall's bricks and mortar were long ago demolished, its spirit and influence remained embodied in a malign and pervasive political machine of seemingly indestructable dimensions. Synonymous since the early 19th Century with the more spectacular forms of municipal graft, greed and corruption, Tammany was nonetheless born out of the American struggle for life, liberty and the pursuit of happiness.

Patriots in New York yearning for independence from Britain showed their derision for loyalist organizations like the St. George Society and the Order of St. Andrew by "canonizing" Tamanend, a legendary chief of the Delaware Indians. Affectionately known thereafter as St. Tammany, he presided over the spirit of revolt as the patron saint of a number of associations called the Sons of St. Tammany. With the War of Independence won and the British gone from New York, however, the Sons of St. Tammany were elbowed from power by wealthy Tory landowners ranged under the banner of the Federalist Party. In 1789 the disgruntled patriots reformed their own ranks as the Society of St. Tammany, which took for its motives, according to a newspaper of the day, "charity and brotherly love".

The Society adopted an outlandish paraphernalia of passwords, secret handshakes and ritual derived from Indian lore, and had as its official chief or Grand Sachem William Mooney, a Manhattan furniture dealer who designated New York the Number One Great Wigwam. Mooney got the show on the road, but Aaron Burr, a suave, handsome and successful New York lawyer of impeccable Teutprot ancestry, provided its star quality.

Burr had fought with gallantry during the War of Independence, receiving promotion to lieutenant-colonel when he was only 21. Never one to hide his light under a bushel, he responded by sending a message to General Washington asking why the promotion had taken so long.

Elected to the New York State Assembly in 1784, Burr quickly distinguished himself as a champion of liberal causes, and by the time the Society of St. Tammany appeared on the scene, he already had a useful

In office for 12 years, Fiorello La Guardia was perhaps the most popular mayor New York has ever had. In this photograph, taken on January 1, 1946, upon his retirement due to ill-health, he waves goodbye to City Hall with the exuberant panache that—together with his strongly reformist programme—recommended him for so long to the voters of the city.

following among New York's underprivileged. Shrewd, ambitious and persuasive, Burr set about turning the braves of Tammany from a group of disaffected political dilettantes into an effective electoral force.

The property qualification for the franchise in the early 19th Century gave the wealthy Federalists a built-in electoral advantage, and so Tammany led the campaign against the property qualification. Meanwhile, to even the balance, Burr arranged bank loans for potential supporters, enabling them to qualify for the vote. In true Tammany style, he also built up an elaborate card index of voters, containing their personal and political histories and indicating how best they could be got to the polls.

In 1791, at the age of 35, he was elected to the U.S. Senate. Taking a leading part in the opposition to President Washington on Capitol Hill, Burr helped Thomas Jefferson weld various anti-Federalist groups into what would become the Democratic Party, and when Jefferson contested the Presidency in 1800, Burr was his Vice-Presidential running-mate. Although the prevailing rules required electors to cast their votes without indicating which office the candidates should hold, it was assumed by the party leaders, including Burr himself, that Jefferson would gain a majority and thus the Presidency. But even Burr had underestimated the strength of his own machine. Both men received exactly the same number of votes, and it was left to Congress to settle the final outcome.

In just over a decade, therefore, Tammany had established itself as a potent political force, not only in New York but in the young American nation at large, and the Number One Great Wigwam was within an ace of seeing its favourite son installed in the White House. Burr, however, was not without enemies, and of these the most dangerous and implacable was Alexander Hamilton. As leader of the New York Federalists and George Washington's chief political adviser, Hamilton declared it his "religious duty" to thwart the young Senator. Hamilton detested Jefferson, but he was appalled by Burr whom he called "as unprincipled and dangerous a man as any country can boast".

Hamilton's desperate attempt to prevent Burr from acceding to the Presidency inspired Sidney Kingsley's fine Broadway drama of 1943, *The Patriots*. Certainly, no work of pure fiction could have contrived the conflict and suspense that built up on Capitol Hill during those first bitter weeks of February, 1801. Hamilton implored, cajoled, bullied, manoeuvred, lobbied and plotted to secure Burr's defeat, and after 36 successive ballots Congress eventually broke the deadlock in favour of Jefferson. As the runner-up, Burr could not be denied the Vice-Presidency, but the office conferred no real power and the new President, alarmed by the recent threat to his own career, excluded Burr and his braves from the fruits of patronage. Three years later Burr lost his campaign for the governorship of New York and also learned that he was to be dropped as the party's Vice-Presidential candidate at the forthcoming elections.

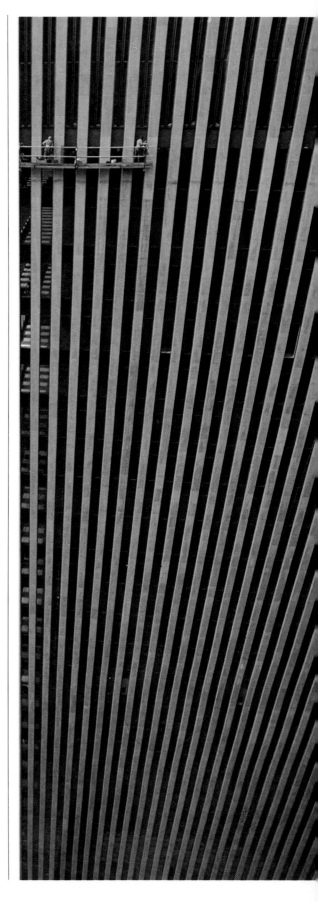

Two workmen, reduced to specks against the striated side of the 54-storey Exxon Building in Rockefeller Center, caulk the limestone piers separating the windows. Men on scaffolds clean the glass on the first six floors; above that level an automatic window-washing machine slides down the building from the top.

A prime mover in all these defeats was, of course, Alexander Hamilton, and when Burr heard that Hamilton had remarked at a supper party that he held a "despicable opinion" of Burr, the Tammany chief's frustrations overwhelmed him. He challenged Hamilton to a duel, and shot his old enemy dead. Burr avoided a murder charge and returned to Washington to complete his term as Vice-President, but in 1806 he was arrested and accused of treason for allegedly plotting to set up an empire in the American West, with New Orleans as the capital and himself as ruler. A jury acquitted him, but Burr was politically ruined. The golden days as Big Chief of the Number One Great Wigwam were over. The political machine that Burr had built was still intact, however, and there were plenty of other Tammany Hall stars waiting in the wings.

The Tammany ethos was succinctly stated in the 1830s on the floor of the U.S. Senate by Senator William Marcy of New York: "It may be that the politicians of New York are not so fastidious as some gentlemen are. They boldly preach what they practise. When they are contending for victory, they avow their intention of enjoying the fruits of it. If they fail, they will not murmur. If they win, they expect to reap all the advantages. They see nothing wrong in the rule, that to the victors belong the spoils of the enemy."

Having succeeded in their own struggle to find a place in the sun, the prospering Teutprot braves of Tammany felt no irresistible urge to exert themselves on behalf of a new and rapidly growing class of New York underprivileged: the Irish immigrants. But the Irish, unwilling to have any truck with the pro-British Federalists, turned naturally to the Democrats, and finding the gates of Tammany Hall locked against them—physically as well as metaphorically—they stormed the place on April 24, 1817, smashing doors, windows, furniture and the heads of the incumbent braves.

The experience was not lost on the Tammany chieftains. The secret of their success had always been their populist appeal and they quickly realized that the clamorous newcomers could provide them with a massive and inexhaustible reservoir of support, particularly if the newcomers acquired the vote. Thus emerged Tammany's enduring and often notorious Irish Connection, and Democratic rededication to the principle of universal manhood suffrage.

In 1821 the New York State Legislature approved an extended franchise and thus ushered in the age of "the Boss", the Tammany chief who was sometimes mayor and always a power in the city and the state. In a nation not averse to individual initiative and private enterprise, the Tammany bosses set new standards of swindling and rapacity. Preserving their electoral stranglehold through a combination of patronage and demagogy, they ruled New York like medieval robber barons. And like robber barons, they sometimes called their bands of armed retainers into action. Neighbourhood gangs such as the Dead Rabbits, the Spartans and the O'Connell Guards acquired semi-official status as Democratic ward committees and

"Boss" Tweed (left) is parodied as a bloated Roman emperor sitting among the ruins of his fallen empire after an 1871 election defeat.

A Ring of Rogues

In the 1860s New York City's treasury was plundered of almost $200 million by the notorious Tweed Ring, a coterie of four corrupt politicians: A. Oakey Hall, Peter "Brains" Sweeny, Richard "Slippery Dick" Connolly and their burly leader, William Marcy Tweed (left). All belonging to the political organization known as Tammany Hall, the four swindlers occupied and financially exploited key civic offices, draining coffers by such brazen ruses as padded bills, payrolls and contracts.

Anti-Tweed crusades were stoked by Thomas Nast's barbed cartoons in *Harper's Weekly*, four of which are reproduced here. But not until the full dimensions of the Ring's crooked activities were exposed did public outrage bring the men to trial in 1871, thus ending their reign of thievery.

All fingers ultimately lead to "Boss" Tweed in a cartoon blaming him for the exorbitant cost involved in building the County Courthouse.

In a royal analogy, Nast suggests that the "king" of Tammany is but a puppet controlled by Tweed, drawn with a sword labelled "Power".

OCTOBER 29, 1870.]

HARPER'S WEEKLY.

THE TAMMANY

KING-DOM

THE POWER BEHIND THE THRONE.

HE CANNOT CALL HIS SOUL HIS OWN.

Th. Nast.

The wind of reformism (left) has blown down Tammany Hall—the bastion of Tweed's power. Tweed lies in the centre fanned by friends.

worked manfully at the polling booths during elections—spurring on Tammany's supporters and deterring its opponents.

Not surprisingly, the division of spoils tended to provoke unseemly behaviour between the barons, and so, in the 1840s, Captain Isaiah Rynders, Tammany boss of the Sixth Ward and head of the Five Points gangsters, took on the task of reconciliation. A former Mississippi riverboat gambler, Captain Rynders was skilled in the use of fist, boot, billy club, knife and pistol, and with the aid of loyal lieutenants like Dirty Face Jack and Country McCleester—and the occasional application of a red-hot poker—he tried to imbue his colleagues with a sense of decorum.

Tammany, of course, did not have things all its own way, and over the years a rough and ready balance emerged: New Yorkers, it seems, can take a modicum of corruption and a modicum of virtue, but not a vast load of either. Boss William Tweed, just after the Civil War, was corrupted and corruptive. He appointed both Mayor and Governor, and he and his cronies—the so-called Tweed Ring—embezzled $200 million of public funds before they were arrested. ("To be a citizen of New York is a disgrace," noted one outraged taxpayer in his diary. "The New Yorker belongs to a community worse governed by lower and baser blackguard scum than any city in Western Christendom.")

Following the Tweed debacle, Tammany's fortunes were restored by the reformist word-mongering of "Honest John" Kelly. A church-going Catholic who owned a soap factory, Boss Kelly promised the people probity and good government and gave them nepotism and knavery. He was said to be worse than Tweed, but on a smaller scale. His successor, a pugnacious Irish pugilist named Richard Croker who had proved his organizing ability as a juvenile gang leader and had, in later life, managed to win acquittal on a murder charge, was so corrupt that he created a reformist backlash. But at the next election the men who had been thrown out were put back in again on the strength of their "To hell with reform" slogan.

The Tammany boss should always, in terms of the power-dividing philosophy on which America was built, have been a bad thing. Yet empirically he was sometimes a good thing. Boss Charles Murphy, who reigned from 1901 to 1923, had a passion for governmental efficiency and a distinct if not entirely disinterested sympathy for the underdog. It was his protege Al Smith who, as Governor of New York, initiated the most far-reaching programme of social reform in the state's history.

Smith's own candidate as Mayor of New York, "Gentleman Jim" Walker, gave the people a one-man circus rather than civic progress, delighting them with his sartorial elegance (he changed his spats and tailored double-breasted suits thrice daily), his amours, his wisecracks ("A reformer is a guy who rides through a sewer in a glass-bottomed boat") and his musical compositions, which included *After They Gather the Hay* and *Will You Love me in December as You Do in May?* The personification of New York

A hell to be endured, New York's subway system consists of grim stations such as this one and is crowded, noisy and dirty. But with 461 stations and 230 miles of track, it is still the quickest, most efficient way to get about.

City during the gay, gaudy Twenties, Walker killed the so-called Clean Books Bill with the comment, "I never heard of a man or woman who was ruined by a book", and once escaped a gambling raid disguised as a waiter.

But in 1932 financial scandal forced Gentleman Jim to resign and the hero of *Fiorello* won the next year's election. A determined anti-Tammany man, Fiorello La Guardia possessed many of the qualities of the traditional Boss, which probably explains why he managed to stave off Tammany Hall and stay the course as Mayor for three successive terms, from 1933 to 1945.

He started his political career in 1916 as a Republican Congressman, but then, with America's entry into the First World War, became an aeroplane pilot—a fact that La Guardia Airport bids us remember. Upon his re-election to Congress after the war his work was altogether progressive: he fought against excessive expenditure on defence, supported women's suffrage, advocated laws to benefit organized labour. As Mayor of New York he was similarly liberal, apparently impervious to corruption and also highly colourful. Once, during a newspaper strike, he read comics over the radio. When Nazis visited New York, he gave them a Jewish police escort. During a coal strike he expedited negotiations by turning the heat off in the room where the disputants were uselessly bickering. He knew many languages; as a young man working for American consulates, he had lived in Hungary, Yugoslavia and Italy. He had a quick wit and a light touch, as befitted his nickname "Little Flower", which is what Fiorello means. He had, in fact, a Bossist panache, a capacity for convincing the citizens that he was "fighting City Hall" with them.

La Guardia was unique, for New York is harder to govern, so it is said, than the entire Union. Although no New York mayor had so far achieved the Presidential chair, even a Roosevelt or a Truman would find it difficult to succeed as a leader of this mixed, turbulent and volatile city. More than administrative genius is required. The Mayor has to have charm and personal force less aristocratic than raffish. He needs to have the glamour out of which Broadway musicals can be made.

Personality is what matters: it offers the only way of slicing through the complexities of the power structure and the political alignments. New York's governmental system is, I suspect, baffling to anyone but an expert. The only guide I can offer is this: the Mayor, as a sort of president figure, has an administrative body known as the Board of Estimate, and a parliament, known as the City Council. Beyond this the administration is a turmoil of ever-changing councils and agencies and boards and commissions and bureaus, of interlocking and redividing responsibilities, of direct and proportional electoral systems that enable the citizens to vote for any number of candidates, in hundreds of posts, and on matters often so arcane that only those who stand to profit can comprehend the issues or care about the result.

Beyond this spongy administrative edifice, the Mayor must also cope with the elected presidents of the various boroughs, with the state of which his city is a part, with the two neighbouring states of Connecticut and New Jersey, to which the city is connected and from which commuters pour in daily by the hundred thousand, and with Washington. And beyond all this again, he must contend with local politics, in particular with a Democratic organization, still very powerful although it no longer has the name, reputation, unity or influence of the old Tammany Hall.

A large majority of the New York City electorate is Democratic, a small minority is Republican. It has always been difficult for a European, and probably also for many an American, to attach precise ideological meaning to this opposition of creeds. In Britain, it is possible to distinguish between Conservatives, Liberals and Socialists under many parameters, but the nature of each of the two major American parties differs from state to state; there are progressive and reactionary elements in both, and like can call to like across the great nominal barriers. La Guardia, for example, was elected as a "Fusion" candidate, backed by Republicans, Liberals, anti-Tammany Democrats and progressive labour organizations; in 1966 liberal Republican John Lindsay won the mayoralty with strong Democratic support. As the pattern of American life is based on upward mobility, there are few levellers on the European models and Marxism is a lost cause.

In spite of all this, New York's Democratic Party remains what it was made to become by the first Irish settlers—the one political body that speaks and acts for the underprivileged. These were once the Irish, the

Italians and the Jews, but now they are the blacks and the Puerto Ricans. While ensuring that the three major religions—Catholic, Jewish and Protestant—all have adequate civic representation, the party also sponsored the first blacks and Puerto Ricans to win elective office in the city.

Although factional in-fighting and the introduction of a social welfare system that made the old-style political boss redundant helped destroy the Tammany political machine in the 1950s, patronage is still an essential element of the New York scene. Everyone is in on the pie. The Mayor himself appoints through patronage. The payroll of his agencies amounts to some $35 million a year and with about a quarter of a million people on the city's own payroll, the opportunities for private aggrandizement are immense. The appointment of judges, district attorneys, high officials of all kinds comes into the patronage system. To get an urban renewal contract or to gain immunity from rent controllers and building inspectors may well involve being friendly with a politician, and friendship is best manifested through generosity.

It is a terrible system, of course, and it is totally inadequate to the physical problems that confront the city. New Yorkers will tell you that things have never been so bad. New Yorkers will equally tell you that things cannot go on like this. This is quite true: they will go on in a different way. In 1968, Mayor John Lindsay stated: "The question now is whether we can survive as a city." In 1975 newspapers screamed of imminent collapse.

That crisis arose as the city and the nation began to realize the consequences of New York's unique, longstanding combination of generosity

Bundles of garbage, stacked into an uneven rampart on a Manhattan sidewalk, dwarf a man scurrying by. The city's army of sanitation men uses about 1,100 trucks and 266 mechanical sweepers to collect an average 23,000 tons of garbage every day from the five boroughs— more than seven million tons each year.

and inefficiency. New York in the early 1970s was spending nearly $8 billion a year on a vast range of services, including schools, libraries, parks, hospitals and a quarter of a million university students (New York alone of American cities has a public university system). Its outlay per head of population was about $1,000 a year—roughly twice as much as any other American city. Population had declined slightly through the 1960s, but the number of public employees had risen by about 100,000 (no one knew the exact figure because controls were so lax).

Moreover, public employees were treated lavishly—a policeman or fireman could retire on half pay after 20 years of service; in 1975, a subway coin changer could make as much as $13,000 a year; bus drivers worked an eight-hour day but were paid for 11 (the three off-peak hours in the middle of the day were their own). Twelve per cent of the population was on welfare, which cost $2 billion a year, five million of which was thought to be lost through fraud. Payrolls were padded. There was one story of a city employee whose job was to answer questions on city affairs by telephone; he admitted that he would take the phone off the hook on arrival in the office and replace it again when he left. Outgoings had long exceeded income, with expenses climbing and income declining. In the early 1970s, pensions alone were costing the taxpayers a totally unproductive $750 million a year.

Faced with an accumulated deficit of more than $950 million, the City authorities instituted a policy of savage retrenchment, and in 1976 Mayor Abraham Beame announced that the city would actually be cutting its spending for the first time since the Depression of the 1930s. The closure of nine of the city's 15 municipal hospitals—designed to serve the poor—and 50 health centres was planned; construction work on 46 city projects, including libraries, police stations and recreation centres, was halted; and 35,000 municipal workers, including 14,000 teachers and 5,000 policemen, were sacked.

But the cuts threatened to create more financial and social problems than they solved. Although the citizens of New York are proud to call themselves children of capitalism, they have grown used to demanding services more appropriate to a heavily socialized state, and when those services could no longer be provided increasing numbers of the affluent middle classes, on whose wealth the city relied, began moving out, while low-income immigrants, often in need of welfare, took their place.

Companies, too, moved out, diminishing the city's tax base and creating more unemployed to burden the welfare services. In the mid-1960s, nearly 200 of the country's top thousand businesses had their headquarters in Manhattan; ten years later, 40 per cent of them had moved elsewhere, and half a million jobs had vanished. In 1976 unemployment in the city had risen to 12.2 per cent—its highest since the Second World War—compared with the national average of 7.8 per cent, and some estimates put

Automobile headlamps add an eerie glare to a cloud of steam escaping into the street from a manhole. The clouds are due sometimes to leaks in steam mains, sometimes to rainwater seepage evaporating as it strikes the scalding-hot underground pipes. Running under New York's streets, the huge mains carry steam to 2,500 customers for central heating in offices, apartments, hotels and hospitals.

unemployment among the blacks and Puerto Ricans as high as 50 per cent.

To a European there is a quality of fractious infantilism in the city—more often endearing than offensive. When snow falls in Europe it often lies until a thaw is ready to deal with it. Snow falls on New York, and citizens scream for the resignation of their Mayor if he does not clear their streets in a week. They throw away an average 23,000 tons of rubbish daily and grumble that the streets are not clean. The cost of transporting water to the city is very high, since it has to come from many parts of the state and from distances up to 300 miles, and yet New Yorkers think nothing of consuming on average one-and-a-half billion gallons a day.

The ultimate in infantilism, although only a tiny majority of New Yorkers indulged in it, was the disfiguring of public transport with graffiti, which cost the city half a million dollars in ineffectual cleaning. The fire department gets two hoax calls for every genuine one. The air is polluted and millions have to be spent on preventive research. New Yorkers abuse their environment as children break their toys; then they scream.

They do not scream when they should. American man is sometimes called *Homo automobilis*, and there seems to be a deep conviction, in New York as everywhere, that a demand for a well-run public transport system is sinful, a kind of breaking of a Mosaic covenant with General Motors. If a man is not getting around in his own car, then he ought to be made to suffer. Manhattan has far too many cars—more than 100 million annually pass through New York's tunnels and across the bridges. But the tolls that are gathered go to the Port Authority, not to the city (the Port Authority does pass on some of the money for improvement of public transport). There are more than 200 miles of subway, which an investigatory committee appointed by Mayor Lindsay described as "dank, dingily lit, fetid, raucous, one of the world's meanest transit facilities".

But to ride the subway, risking death and a large measure of aesthetic affront, may be preferable to commuting with a quarter of a million other passengers on the six railroads that link Manhattan to the suburbs. I used to travel regularly between Princeton Junction, New Jersey and Manhattan, and can attest to a quantity of discomforts and hazards that commuters had come to tolerate with the stoicism of long habituation: failed air conditioning, sudden black-outs, delays and accidents, stones and even bullets fired at sinful Teutprot passengers by fractious blacks.

One aspect of the apparently unchangeable inefficiency of which I have a deep personal experience is education. The purpose of education is to transmit culture, and New York City is heavily committed to the provision of schooling at all levels, with—according to most observers—a poor return for a heavy annual outlay of $1.5 billion. Carpers complain of lack of discipline, drug-pushing even in elementary schools, an inadequate curriculum, low status for teachers. A system devoted to monetary profit has never been able to see how teachers, who produce nothing marketable, justify their existence. Well-qualified men of powerful athletic prowess and great pedagogic ability have been stigmatized as "male school-marms".

Few in America seem to regard the instruction of the young as a vocation, and it requires a brave (or foolish) man or woman to face a multi-racial mob in a New York elementary school. Moreover, the general lack of an educational philosophy puts teachers in the position of not knowing what they are doing or why. Even at the university level there is too often an over-willingness to please rather than instruct, a scorn for the past, a doubt of the value of literacy. Many of the supposed educators either express themselves through slang or self-indulgent twaddle like this (a teacher's report on a slow learner's allocation to a slow learners' class): "His grade placement under the multiple-track plan reflects his predisposition to those factors frequently associated with late bloomers lacking the development key of meaningful motivation and without the felt need to effectuate the tasks involved in the learning process." (In other words: "He is in a low class because he is slow and lazy.")

A central policy for New York education should be simple enough and should be concerned primarily with language. For good or ill, the common tongue of New York is English. To live in New York is to commit oneself to such mastery of the language as will enable one to cope with communication outside one's own ethnic group: to use English as a *lingua franca*. To bring up a family in New York means committing one's children to attempted mastery of the language that Washington, Jefferson and Martin Luther King used. To burble over the ghetto dialect known as "black English", enthusing over its ingenious syntax and expressive beauties, as some progressive whites do, is to laud a deprived language. To opt out of English is to opt out of New York and America.

Anxious to be just to the underprivileged, New York has been prepared to see elementary, high school and university standards adjusted to the capabilities of the slower learners. I took a post as a teacher of fiction writing in City College when the system of open admission was instituted. This meant the relaxation of formerly exacting entrance standards, and its true aim was not educational, but political, enabling more blacks and Puerto Ricans to gain a university education. Because of the financial crisis, entrance requirements were reinstated in 1976, and the students admitted were generally better qualified, but still not as academically well prepared as their European counterparts.

Professor William Riley Parker, of Indiana University, said in 1961: "There is not a single assumption that I as a teacher of graduate students in English can make about either the knowledge or skill they have already supposedly acquired. I cannot assume knowledge of the simplest Bible story or myth or fairy tale or piece of children's literature."

This has been pretty well my own experience, in New York and else-where. It is very American to assume that the past does not exist, that history, in Henry Ford's memorable if nonsensical dictum, is bunk. The attainments of New York's graduates are not matched by the facilities still available to them. The stone lions on 42nd Street and Fifth Avenue guard one of the great libraries of the world. The special libraries at the Lincoln Center, at Columbia (the Low Memorial), the Pierpont Morgan Library—all are magnificent. New York is also notable for its museums—private, but mostly helped by the city to the tune of $18 million a year—and its art collections. All these are amenities as vital as zoos and parks and beaches. The city should never be without them. But like so many other things that strain the city's limited resources, they are, in a financial sense, pure loss.

In the long run, New Yorkers will get what they want—and what they want may well include a filthy subway and an inefficient municipal apparatus. They know what goes on and they have the power of choice. Their sources of information are not, like their air and waterways, polluted. I have been in the biggest territory of the British Commonwealth—Australia—and in one of the smallest—Malta (now a republic)—and have suffered from censorship to a degree unthinkable in New York.

In New York you may see what films you wish, and you are free to read the books of your choice. New York's journalists and broadcasters are the fairest in the world and its critics of the arts are both elegant and well-informed. Sometimes freedom of the written or spoken word is abused—in the sense that obscenity is exploited for its own sake and not in the interests of an aesthetic or moral end. But this is a reflection on individuals, not on the basic climate of free expression. The civic mess is not hidden; whatever happens, the citizen can become involved, and this is an invaluable asset to set against inefficiency and corruption.

What actually will happen in the years ahead is anyone's guess. Mayor Lindsay once told Congress that it would cost $8 billion a year to put the city right. The figure must have increased drastically since then, and is rising daily. Failing a solution, the city could always put itself up for auction. Perhaps the Arabs would be willing to take over the city, pulling down the Statue of Liberty as an image inadmissable to Islam, closing the bars, and having renamed New York "New Mecca", hoisting the flag of the star and sickle moon over the World Trade Center. The Jews would object, of course, but such changes would be short-term. New Mecca would absorb its conquerors and convert them to amiable corruption, pizza, gefilte fish and the delights of Radio City. Fantasy aside, I will make my own confession of faith: New York *will* survive. It is an aspect of America that America cannot do without. Nobody can do without it.

The Vitality of the Street

PHOTOGRAPHS BY LEONARD FREED

In a time-honoured summer game of the New York streets, a grinning boy rakes the full width of the road with a powerful jet of water from a city fire hydrant.

With all its much publicized social and financial problems, New York may sometimes seem from a distance almost like a city under siege. But a walk through the neighbourhoods of Manhattan on a hot weekend in summer shows another New York, a city where the vigorous life of the streets continues unaffected by any sense of threat. Different areas have their own distinct character: the sidewalks of the lower East Side are crowded with Puerto Ricans idling away a warm evening; on Upper Broadway political activists solicit signatures on petitions; Greenwich Village on a Saturday afternoon is alive with fund-raising bazaars put on by local groups. But common to all these various districts and their inhabitants is a natural vitality and a capacity for extemporized gaiety that give expression to the very human side of New York.

Unself-consciously proud of his eye-catching elegance, an athletic young Puerto Rican stands with easy grace on top of the heaped-up garbage on the sidewalk.

Lounging nonchalantly, a brawny Greenwich Villager chats with neighbours at a party held on his street.

Kings of the Walk

All the human relationships of a small community are played out during summer in the streets, which in New York often serve the purpose of both back gardens and parks. Parents gossip, children play, and with the sense of relaxation and confidence born of being on their own territory, young men casually posture for passers-by. Out of elements like these the indefinable life of many a local neighbourhood is composed.

Overflowing on to the sidewalk to escape
from the airless heat of their crowded
apartments, a group of Puerto Ricans on the
lower East Side greet with easy hilarity the
diverting antics of a cigar-smoking granny.

With a block party in full swing in the street below, a small group of friends enjoy a leisurely glass of wine on the steps of a house in Greenwich Village.

Among the milling crowd at a street fair, passers-by join in with a team of Morris dancers whose performance constitutes part of the afternoon's programme.

Life in the Open

Block parties—street bazaars put on by the residents of one or more streets to raise money for amenities like playgrounds or tree-planting—provide welcome outdoor entertainments during the hot-weather months. Scarcely a weekend in summer passes without a block party taking place somewhere in Manhattan, the style of the occasion—formal and gracious or noisy and gay—depending on the character of the neighbourhood where it is being held.

Under the black side of a freighter docked at the Hudson River waterfront near Greenwich Village, families in shirt-sleeves and bathing suits spend the afternoon on a wharf opened to the public by its owners. Gritty and black though the ground may be, they sit contentedly in the sun, for New Yorkers gravitate to any open space that will allow them to catch a cooling breeze and pick up a tan.

7

The Worst and the Best

George Orwell said that a good society would preserve an old slum or two —not to show how bad life had been in the past but, in spite of everything, how good it had been. I lived in a slum district of Manchester, England, until I joined the army at 21 and look back upon a life there that was poor indeed but also rich, friendly, dramatic, vivid, never boring.

The old "ethnic" slums of New York were like that. They bred an energy, a capacity for self-expression that could realize ambition. They were not permanent centres of hopelessness but posting-stations on the way up. Not for all, of course. But even for those who stayed behind there were sustaining values. Such slums, being centred on a single race and language and culture, had a unity of sensibility and conduct, and could even develop leaders, spokesmen, voices of aspiration. There was rowdiness, but not much violence. Some people became prosperous enough to move to the suburbs, but they would sometimes stay on out of attachment to friends, a culture, a way of life.

Now all of that is dying. New York's slums are changing and there is less hopefulness in the city and among its citizens. The problems are enormous and the "solutions" do not seem to work. New York has become in many ways a terrible and frightening place. And yet I love it, as do millions of others—a paradox, but one that I hope to show is not so unreasonable as at first it may appear.

A characteristic of many New York slums today is racial integration: whites and blacks moving among shops with Hebrew lettering, the recorded sound of Hispanic music, the smell of *knockwurst*. Nonetheless, this mix is not evidence of enlightenment; it covers rootlessness and despair. Poverty is a great unifying force, but it provides only a unity of place. The stable family life necessary to keep delinquency in check is disintegrating. The new domestic pattern increasingly is serial relationships: a man and a woman live together, have children, separate and proceed to new co-habitations. What energy there is often is destructive, expressed in anger, in juvenile gangs: the Phantom Lords, the Hell Burners.

The government-financed housing project has been the official answer to the slum tenement. But the number of new units built does not equal the number of old slum-dwellings left to complete ruin or demolished to make way for the new. There never seems to be enough public housing to go around. And slum-dwellers who become project-dwellers are not necessarily happier, cleaner, more law-abiding in their high-rise cells. They are abandoned to the cold impersonality of bureaucracy. There are rigid rules,

Holding a small friend during a block party, a smiling auxiliary police officer—part-time, volunteer policeman who helps the regular force on routine duties—wears evidence of a visit to a fund-raising attraction: a face-painting stall where he earned an extra set of stripes. The black band across his badge is a mark of mourning for two policemen shot dead the day before in the line of duty.

154/ **The Worst and the Best**

checks on violations, a sense of being supervised. As neighbourhoods change, some older tenants withdraw completely—shutting themselves in, losing identity, becoming faceless. Others go in for "bench culture" as they try to maintain contact with their own vanishing ethnic group. There are benches outside the buildings where the Jews sit and talk, other benches for Puerto Ricans, others for blacks: self-elected segregation. And the young go in for violence.

It is violence, of course, that worries New Yorkers most. Violence and theft. To quote from *Another America*, written by a colleague of mine at City University, Geoffrey Wagner: violence "haunts the edge of the New York imagination daily. It rides in the mind each apprehensive subway jolt home . . . when you turn the stiff key in the fourth deadlock latticing your door and switch off the alarm, will it be to find the joint trashed once more, a mess of drawers piled on the floor, the TV set taken again, the curtains bellying mockingly from the window to the fire escape?"

Wagner himself left the city the month his wife lost her third handbag to snatchers and a thief coolly lowered himself through a skylight into his office while he was there. This is an increasingly common run of experience in New York, where about 440,000 felonies are committed annually. Every week in London a woman is raped (not always the same woman); but ten are raped daily, on average, in New York. More than 70,000 cars are stolen annually in and around the city. Of still worse crimes, there are some 1,600 murders a year, roughly compared to a hundred in London.

It was not always like this. Senior citizens remember three decades— from the 1920s to the 1940s—when, in spite of Prohibition, the Depression, and political scandals of all kinds, it was possible to live with unlocked doors or, on a hot night, sleep unmolested in Central Park.

Those days are gone, perhaps forever. There is now an element in New York life that has not always been there: the drug cult, in ranker flower than anywhere else in the Union. Junkies, who desperately need large sums of money regularly to support their demanding addictions and will take it any way they can get it, are mainly responsible for the vast increase in mugging and burglary.

Traffic in illegal drugs is almost impossible to extinguish because it has become such a big and lucrative business. Diacetylmorphine, commonly known as heroin, is one of the great commodities of New York. A kilo of pure, imported heroin when diluted and sold in small quantities on the street may generate a profit of as much as 1,000 per cent. The trade of supplier, which requires no training, is taken up at a very early age by calculating non-users; lisping dope-sellers operate even in elementary school lavatories. It is not unusual for a really professional dope-dealer to gross $50,000 in a day and to become a millionaire in two years. The big men at the top, importers and wholesalers, obviously make much more.

Holding a sheaf of identification photographs, an officer of the homicide squad questions West Side residents for possible clues to a recent murder. In 1975 some 1,600 homicides were committed in New York and the police made more than 1,200 arrests in the course of their investigations.

Mention of the drug business requires mention of the Mafia, an organization of Sicilian origin. Its function in Sicily was to act as an alternative government, or to replace in effect a government not much concerned with governing—such as the colonial one half-heartedly put in by the Spaniards who once ruled Sicily. Many Sicilians when they first came to America assumed that an Anglo-Saxon system of laws was like a colonial Sicilian one, and that it was as necessary for the Mafia to operate in New York as in Palermo. Anglo-Saxon law has proved ineffective enough to allow the modern, efficient, well-disciplined Mafia to gross an estimated $20 billion to $50 billion a year in the United States.

Much of that impressive income used to come from illegal narcotics. But after the heroin shortage of the early 1970s, due primarily to the restriction on the growth of Turkish poppies (and the increased effort of the French police to shut down laboratories in Marseilles), the Mafia lost its dominant role in the drug trade to blacks and Hispanic Americans who got their supplies from Asia and Latin America.

Mafiosi have now concentrated increasingly on gambling (an activity of which New York, in spite of its restrictive laws, has always been tolerant), and on muscling into respectable enterprises: banking, union organizations, trucking, construction, restaurants, bakeries, laundries. That is not to say they participate in these businesses in a legitimate manner, whatever surface impression is promoted by gang chieftains with costly homes in tranquil suburban communities and children in college. Their technique is still basically extortion; their tool, force.

New Yorkers may shrug off organized crime as a fact of life, like smog.

They cannot so easily shrug off the drug-rooted violence that is at least in part a Mafia legacy, one of the organization's enduring contributions to New York amenities. True, they can joke about it. Everyone has his favourite mugging story. A man leaving his house to post a letter is mugged, begins one such anecdote. On his return another mugger accosts him.

"You're too late," says the man. "Someone got me on my way out."

"What did he look like?" demands the mugger, aggrieved. "This is my block!"

New Yorkers laugh, but they also take defence measures that reach fantastic lengths. Door locks are doubled, trebled, quadrupled. Closed-circuit TV cameras scan the corridors of apartment buildings, monitored in entrance lobbies by guards—some with guns. Windows are protected by iron bars. Citizens volunteer to spend non-working hours as auxiliary policemen, covering their beats in private prowl cars. Women clutch their handbags tightly when they go shopping and wear whistles round their necks in case they need to summon help.

If confirmed Manhattan dwellers have finally begun to leave in increasing numbers, they can hardly be blamed. But residents, nonetheless, are generally less prone to be appalled by the threat of sudden, senseless violence than are visitors. Many New Yorkers seem to have developed a Mithridates-like immunity to fear; King Mithridates of Asia Minor inoculated himself with all the poisons of the world and hence ate and drank freely of whatever was set before him. He died old. People in New York, inoculated by experience, walk on the sidewalk's edge away from shadows, avoid parks and certain streets; and when an outsider asks if the city is safe, they reply with disdain that of course it is—if he knows where to walk.

A tense city, and yet I thrive in it. For violence is only one side of the coin. Dante's Florence, too, was violent and so was Shakespeare's London. In a totally tranquil city you will find dusty ideas and no art; human energy can erupt in an offence against a person or his property, but it can also do so in a symphony. New York's destructive dynamism has its mirror-image: a dynamism that is creative, ever-moving, self-renewing.

Buckminster Fuller described New York as a "continual evolutionary process of evacuations, demolitions, removals, temporarily vacant lots, new installations and repeat. This process is identical in principle to the annual rotation of crops in farm acreage—plowing, planting the new seed, harvesting, plowing under, and putting in another type of crop."

This is true. New York thrives on newness. One has to give a reason in New York for not changing but not for changing. The new does not have to be novel; it merely has to be something that was not there before. The resulting impermanence of the townscape—as well as the quick changes in manners, fashions, tastes—should probably appal me. Things are made to last in England, where the past is sometimes more alive than the present.

In Search of Security

In New York, where reported burglaries reach almost 200,000 a year (a small proportion of the real total), harried police admit they have to give break-ins about the same priority as noise complaints. Some New Yorkers, who can afford the outlay, fit their apartments with sophisticated anti-burglar systems, but most householders settle for fixing a variety of more or less ingenious locks

in their efforts to deter unwelcome visitors.

Top left, a bicycle lock secures the window catches; bottom left, the protection of assorted bolts and padlocks is belied by a vulnerable pane mended with tape; top right, an accordion gate defends a ramshackle window accessible via a fire escape; bottom right, strands of barbed wire decorate a spike-studded wall.

I once lived in Adderbury, in Oxfordshire, where the rustics spoke of the pranks of the Earl of Rochester (1647-1680) as fairly recent history. I left and lived abroad for six years. On my return the local postman said: "Hello, Misterrr Burrrgess, you bin on yer 'olidies'?" My wife, being Italian, is even more tied to the past and, like Italy itself, cannot bear to throw anything away (we have a battered fork that she rescued from a 57th Street garbage can). Nevertheless, she and I have an equal love of this changeful city.

We recognize how salutary it is to be compelled to live in the present. After all, the past—however glamorous—is a burden. To be forced to lug around both a past and a future is to have one's existential freedom taxed. New York is, in a sense, the future; so the future does not really have to concern it. It tries not to acknowledge the past, except when the past can, as in some historical film or pageant, be seen as merely a piquantly dressed-up version of the present. European neuroses often have to do with the incubus of the past and the hopelessness of the future; New York neuroses spring from present pressures. When I feel suicidal in Europe, it is mostly because of a sense of past failure—in art and human reactions alike. In New York such gloom rarely oppresses me: yesterday is dead.

The removal of the guilt of the past means, to an Englishman, the removal also of certain irrelevant standards derived from the past which, in his own country, are used to judge and often to condemn him. In England a man is not always accepted on his merits. The accent with which he speaks is taken as a logarithm of breeding. Ability is never enough. Southern England—with London, Oxford, Cambridge, Eton and Harrow as the centres of power and prestige—is therefore highly oppressive to the British provincial. He has to break into that charmed principality through tricks rather than native ability (Shaw's *Pygmalion* is an allegory of this). He cannot, except in some small sphere like popular music, hope to turn his own provincial centre into a rival to London. He has to get out and build a new and remote capital.

The same applies to the relationship between other provincials in other countries and their leading cities. But provincials of many nations made New York. It represents the achievements of people who were traditionally cut off from the centres of power, men not lying on the great gilded bed of the past but active and about, trying to make meaning out of the present.

Living in the present means living not on memory or even expectation but in the senses and the nerves. In Europe even eating and drinking are somehow acts of communication with the past. This is literally so in France, where some country soup-kettles have simmered away since the time of Richelieu. To eat chicken Marengo is to be eucharistically linked with a Napoleonic victory. In China things go further; an egg may be kept in the family for untold centuries and be eaten on a ceremonial occasion.

Eating in New York is kept severely in place, an existential function. The city has its great restaurants where one may dine and drink as well and as expensively as in Paris, but the big New York achievement is short-order cookery. A drink is a machine for cooling the throat, injecting speedy sugar into the pancreas, getting high. There is no mystique of the past attached to a Coke or a highball.

Living in the present means cramming the present with all that infinitesimal time-point can take. It means hustle and bustle, although often pointless and sometimes ineffectual. I find New York's vigour endearing for its own sake, even when it is inefficient. No one can bear too much efficiency.

Even the city's corruption is human. New York is full of poor, sinful creatures in all walks of life who simply cannot resist temptation. It is what André Malraux called *la condition humaine*. The New York *condition* gets more *humaine* every day. I was brought up in a tradition of British incorruptibility that was, in those days, more than a myth. I worked as a civil servant in British protectorates where Chinese contractors and shopkeepers were always ready to bribe, but no bribe was ever taken. British policemen, in old *Punch* cartoons, courted the cooks of Belgravia houses and were fed apple-pie. This is as far as British police corruption *ever* traditionally got. New York police often expect more than pie.

Perhaps love of New York, as opposed to liking or merely admiring it, can only be expressed in the very human terms of a neighbourhood. When I lived in an apartment on West End Avenue—that was the building's official address; actually, the entrance was around the corner on West 93rd Street, a fact that was conveniently ignored for the more fashionable listing —I took that environment of very small compass to my bosom, and the environment took me to its. I was always thankful to get back to it by subway from work. When, after some trip to another town in another state, the taxi from La Guardia approached the neighbourhood, my heart lifted: this was home.

Home was more than the stuffy, dark apartment. It was the guard in the vestibule, doing his job in this desperate city, the four closed-circuit telescreens on the look-out for armed intrusion. It was the supermarket around the corner, with its "special offers", its Muzak, and its excessive variety of comestibles. It was the Library Bar and Restaurant, where the walls were covered with books that really were sometimes read, and where the whisky-drinking stranger on the next stool turned out to be an expert on Old English phonology.

It was the Thalia cinema, run-down and already possessed of the haunted look of something about to be demolished; the Cleopatra restaurant for Middle Eastern food; and the countless Chinese restaurants. It was the two cigar stores, which were better stocked with fumable exotica than most of the great hotel-lobby concessions downtown. It was the Sicilian wineshop, whose owner, when the opening of my bank account was long delayed, gladly cashed *lire* cheques on my Rome bank and sent them home to his relations. More than anything, it was the people.

I became one of these people, a New Yorker. My accent was regarded as strange, but New York is built on strange accents.

There was one flaw in my general content, and that of my wife. Our son was eight years old, and it was soon evident that New York was not for him. He was used to the street life of Rome, but no street life was possible here. Being Anglo-Italian, he was vulnerable to unique racial gibes. His bicycle was stolen on the day I bought it for him. He witnessed a bloody maiming at the street corner. His out-of-school life soon was largely limited to watching the innumerable infantile television shows, the programmes for children often being less infantile than the adult ones. It was a life that had to be cosseted and enclosed. When I was offered a permanent professorship at Columbia University, I felt I had to refuse; I had a young and impressionable life to consider.

But this is a minor-key note, and I do not propose to end on it. New York is a city for strong men and women. It fulfils the historic condition for civilized and creative cities. Ben Jonson killed a man with a dagger; Christopher Marlowe died in a tavern brawl; Shakespeare undoubtedly carried a sword. Florence, London and Paris have survived violence, corruption and the other manifestations of original sin. So will New York.

It will survive because, in spite of everything, it is in the hands of its own people. It is the concrete expression of a powerful desire to achieve self-rule, a blessing unknown to so many of its immigrant refugees from oppression. Even the Bossism and graft and, perhaps, the organized gangs (including the Mafia) are aspects of an attempt to contrive a viable polity from the bottom, to avoid an imposed despotism at the top. Its philosophy is mostly concerned with earning a living; and while this single-minded materialism has produced drug-dealers and slum landlords, great beauty has also arisen from it, almost accidently.

New York's skyline is always changing, but it will always be the same: the high towers of the future built in the present. Life in Northampton or Lausanne may be safer, but no city in the world is more enthralling. Wherever we live, we are all proud to be New Yorkers—and, of course, suitably ashamed.

8

The Real Pleasures of Fun City

Along with its horrors, New York offers an unequalled wealth of recreative pleasures. I have not experienced them all, nor could I ever hope to, nor would I ever want to. I have my own peculiarly New York pleasures, and they are quite enough for me. They are not confined to theatres and concert halls but are to be found also in the streets, bars, zoos, museums and—thanks in large part to a 19th-Century American poet—in one of the world's greatest parks.

I do not know whether the poems of William Cullen Bryant are still read. I struggled once with his *Thanatopsis* ("a view of death"—an attractively romantic subject) and understand that children used to be fond of his *Robert of Lincoln*. But, whatever his literary merits, he is a fascinating personage to a European like myself, because in the grand American way, he combined contemplation and action. Hemingway not only wrote of war but waged it himself; Bryant was not only a nature-lover in the romantic tradition but also one of the creators of New York's Central Park.

One of the differences between Europe and America may be stated thus: in Europe things come about and then have to be justified philosophically; in America things are grandly and innocently created out of a philosophy. England's Constitution grew, or accumulated, haphazardly, empirically, without even a scrap of paper to write it on; that of the United States emerged boldly and idealistically, influenced by a treatise on law, *De l'Esprit des lois*, written by the French philosopher Montesquieu. So also William Cullen Bryant, soaked in Wordsworthian nature, loathing the bricks and mortar of towns, started a vigorous and effective campaign in 1844 to enforce a great chunk of unspoiled, God-breathing nature on filthy, corrupt Manhattan.

He was supported, naturally enough, not by politicians but by other writers—the novelist Washington Irving and a historian named George Bancroft. It was a hard struggle but eventually they persuaded the municipality to acquire what was at the time described by a Frenchman as "*une lande dénudée, laide et dégoûtante*"—territory compounded of the disgusting, the filthy, the waste—and to turn it into a civic nature reserve.

It was, in those days, pastoral land after the New York pattern. It was infested by squatters who raised shacks and pigs, milked goats and distilled illicit spirits in bosky hollows. Frederick Law Olmsted, who was to become the chief designer of the park, called it "a pestilential spot, where rank vegetation and miasmatic odours taint every breath of air". For all that, it was expensive territory and its 843 acres cost $5 million to buy.

Garbed in the blue-denim uniform of the young and casual, two New Yorkers set out for a stroll, in which they will tap the boundless resources of the city. For the independent and self-reliant, New York is one of the world's richest and most rewarding cities.

Olmsted was an independently wealthy Staten Island farmer who had achieved some success as a writer, but whose first love was parks. On extensive travels in Europe he had spent most of his time studying them. Parks were, he later wrote, "what I wanted in London and in Paris and in Brussels and everywhere I went". A New York politician suggested that Olmsted apply for the job of superintending the park's development and, with the backing of Washington Irving and William Cullen Bryant, he was appointed to the post.

Olmsted's assignment was to oversee the work, not to plan it, but when the city announced a competition for design of the park in 1857, Calvert Vaux, an architect, persuaded him to collaborate on an entry. Their plan exploited the area's natural topography, emphasizing existing hills and bluffs and included the then novel feature of sunken cross-park roads spanned by bridges so that pedestrians would not have to contend with wheeled traffic. (They also threw an abundance of curves and bends into the roads to discourage carriage racing by young New York blades who were creating a dangerous nuisance with their races on a long, straight stretch of Broadway to the west.) Their scheme, submitted under the pseudonym "Greensward", was selected.

With an army of 3,000 men—mostly immigrant Irishmen who got their jobs through political patronage—and 400 horses, hindered by squatters who hurled stones at the enterprise and its creators (the police had to be called to quell them), they set to work, blasting, digging, shifting, planting. In all some ten million wagonloads of soil and stone were moved, half a million cubic yards of fertilizer were applied, and more than four million trees and bushes were planted. In 1876, almost two decades after it began, the great task was completed, and Central Park had the aspect that it more or less bears today.

In the 19th Century it was essentially "smart", jingling with broughams, victorias and phaetons, enflowered by great ladies exquisitely attired. It was glossy with fine horses. It became fashionable to drive one's own coach and four (or, after a winter snowstorm, one's sleigh) along its avenues. Leonard Jerome, the maternal grandfather of Winston Churchill, founded a Coaching Club of great exclusiveness and distinction. But, as the park was part of New York City, it had to yield sooner or later to the allure of the machine. Bicycles appeared and ladies rode them, to the scandal of the conservative. It was the great and beautiful Lillian Russell who made the bicycle glamorous if not quite respectable: her machine was plated with gold and it bore her monogram in jewels.

The park's guardians put up stronger resistance to the automobile. By 1899 it was the last park in New York that still banned motor cars. The Automobile Club of America made a *cause célèbre* of this infringement of the motorist's freedom to motor, dispatching drivers into Central Park to face certain and well-publicized arrest. The park commissioners yielded.

While her brother clambers up to join her, a girl quietly relishes the special pleasure children derive from perching on Central Park's statue of Hans Christian Andersen. The bronze effigies of the Danish storyteller and his Ugly Duckling have been polished by small admirers' hands and feet since being installed in 1956.

In November, 1899, the first permit was issued to operate an automobile in the park. This was probably the most important defeat suffered in the long and still continuing struggle to preserve Central Park as an island of rustic tranquillity in a sea of urban frenzy.

For Central Park was meant for Byzantian contemplation as much as for motion and display. Its architects were concerned with lakes and trees and flowers. The vegetation, unfortunately, has had to contend with thin soil covering hard rock, but the sweep of grassland where, as late as 1910, sheep used to graze, the thousands of trees and flowering shrubs—these continue to delight in spite of the thugs and vandals. Geese and ducks swim the lakes, and starlings and squirrels take nuts from one's hand. Dogs may not chase them; dogs have to be kept on leashes—although, New Yorkers being New Yorkers, not all are.

This fine stretch, associated these days as much with death and rape as with romantic pleasure, takes up a very large part of Manhattan, flanked by Central Park West and Fifth Avenue and topped and tailed by 110th and Central Park South respectively. It is undeniably central and its shape is as mathematically exact as the United States Constitution. Being American, or New York, it does not merely contain everything that the heart of man could desire, except for guaranteed safety to the person; it contains too much, it is a fearful paradise of excess, like the city that surrounds it.

To start at the bottom right hand—that is, south-eastern—corner, where stands the Grand Army Plaza, you will find hansom cabs for rent. The cabbies were traditionally perky Cockneys who would call you guv'nor, refugees from a London where motor taxis had taken over, and this tradition was maintained in movies about New York during that romantic era that had to be displaced by stark and boring realism.

Then, just inside the confines of the park, there is the Pond, shaped like an old boot, with the Wollman Rink to the north-west of it. I have never ice-skated there, but I have danced. I associate the Rink especially with the square-dancing that used to be held there, which, in over-sophisticated Manhattan, took on a slightly ironic quality, being so much the product of hick and healthy innocence. I regret to say that square-dancing eventually gave way to rock concerts at the Rink.

Then there is the big Heckscher Playground, where there are six softball fields—where horseshoe throwing is also a popular diversion—and a water playground of spraying fountains, wet slides and ankle-deep wading rivulets. In the Sheep Meadow, just north of the Playground, I have attended at least two New York Philharmonic concerts but not yet a concert under the band shell on the adjacent mall. There is, as I say, too much going on. North of the Sheep Meadow is a lake called, with divine simplicity, the Lake, with the Bethesda Fountain and fishing. East of here is a pool for model boating and a statue of Hans Christian Andersen where, on summer Saturday mornings, little stories are told to children sated with television. Then, on the Great Lawn, there is the Delacorte Theatre, where the Shakespeare Festival is held.

There is, indeed, a devotion to Shakespeare in Central Park not accorded to any other poet. Joseph Papp's bizarre productions of *The Two Gentlemen of Verona* and *Much Ado About Nothing*, trendy, updated, bringing Manhattan rowdiness to enliven the staid Bard, were one aspect of the devotion. The other is more touching, more delicate. With Central Park police station to its south, reminding us of the non-Shakespearian world without, a Shakespeare Garden offers a sort of botanical guide to the Stratford nature imagery of the plays.

The huge Receiving Reservoir, big American water, is surrounded by more manly attractions—basketball, soccer, homegrown football, field hockey, jogging, riding, tennis. Up in the North Meadow eight diamonds accommodate baseball. Now, the particular and unique quality of the pleasures to be derived from Central Park lies in the fact that you are aware of the city outside it. Boating on the Lake, you can see sky-scrapers beyond the trees and bushes. A synthetic medieval castle is sternly reminded by the modern monsters that life is real, that there is no escape to dreams of troubadours and chivalry. *Rus* and *urbs*, the timeless and the time-bound, are forced to come to terms, often charmingly.

But it is the city that is really in charge. Amenity is doggedly forced on a great patch of rurality that, as nature left to itself, would be all a William

The entrance hall of the Metropolitan Museum of Art—designed in the grandiose, neo-classical manner of the 1890s—forms part of the central building completed in 1902. The museum's 234 galleries are visited by more than three million people annually, many of them city dwellers who come and go regularly.

Cullen Bryant required. Just as California's Forest Lawn is not content merely to be a resting-place for the dead but has to have pervasive soft music, a stained-glass travesty of Leonardo's "Last Supper", and lubricious statuette souvenirs, so New York's Central Park has to have a zoo (and a very pleasant one, too), a place for chess and checkers, an Alice in Wonderland statue and mounted policemen—as well as some disguised as private citizens on foot or bicycle—prowling after wrongdoers.

It could have been worse. From the park's inception groups and individuals, for motives well-meant or ill, have tried to foist "improvements" on it or carve off pieces for other uses. Had they been successful Central Park would have a Coney-Island-like fun fair, a huge sports stadium, radio transmitting towers, underground parking for 30,000 cars, several additional roads, streetcar tracks, a statue of Buddha and an airport. In the 1930s Mayor La Guardia seriously proposed selling off part of the Fifth Avenue frontage for building development and as late as 1964 the construction of a high-rise housing project was suggested for the park's northernmost end.

Among the most prominent successful invasions of the park's original territory is that of the Metropolitan Museum of Art, which stands south of the Receiving Reservoir fronting Fifth Avenue. There are, I suppose, two things to say about the Metropolitan Museum, apart from conventional panegyrics on its opulence. It is, following the New York metaphysic, excessive. I have walked in often and, as often, walked out again. I have not mastered the cultivated New Yorker's trick of taking in a segment during the half-hour not pre-empted by a business cocktail or a clandestine amour. Aware of all that art, I decide I do not particularly want art.

The other point is that all this magnificence represents a margin of free-enterprise wealth, not a Napoleonic parcel of filched tributes. The great monied names represent the substructure of the incredible beauty displayed: Wall Street and Fifth Avenue names—Morgan, Rockefeller, Altman. The artistic wealth is a tribute to overflowing pockets. This does not, of course, impair the aesthetic experiences the Museum offers. All I can say of them is that they scare me with their fine excess.

On the ground floor, the right and left wings respectively devote themselves to clothes and to children. The Costume Institute appeals to me because it is so frankly related to New York's major trade. It tells the history of clothes in general, but it has much to say about contemporary fashions and it glorifies French and New York couturiers. It is a candid mixture of commerce and aesthetic instruction. The Junior Museum of the opposite wing is not intended to appeal to visitors under six or over 15, and hence I, who am overwhelmed by the Egyptian and Oriental Antiquities, am not at all oppressed by the ingenious dioramas and films and models found there. Art and dead civilizations are brought equally to life for children, and I am glad of the opportunity to be temporarily a child.

Something that American money alone could not buy is what is to be found in the American Wing. Here is a fine display of "colonial" interior decoration, and here also are American painters like Whistler, Sargent and Mary Cassat, not to mention Hopper and Pollock. In spite of the Old World elements (Chippendale furniture in the Verplanck drawing-room imported from Wall Street, Mary Cassat's studentship under French painter Dégas), this is indigenous American taste at its best, and it is only marginally connected with American money.

The Museum of Modern Art, the Frick Collection, the Guggenheim, the smaller displays of wealth and taste that lack a guidebook name—these I am going to be heretical or philistine enough to ignore. Just as I will ignore the varied wonders of the United Nations Building on the East River. For these, to me, are not New York; they are any wealthy city that thinks it has a responsibility to culture; they are products of the world outside. The unique flavour that makes New York Fun City is rather to be tasted in the Radio City Music Hall, which many—unversed in the true meaning of the term, culture—might not be willing to regard as true culture at all, or even regard as a pleasure.

In Radio City Music Hall dance 36 long-legged girls called the Rockettes. Them I cannot find elsewhere, as I can find Monet and Picasso and mummies elsewhere. The Rockettes have been dancing in New York since 1932—not the same ones, of course, as there have been periodic replacements of the group's components. They went to Paris in 1937 for the Exposition and brought three Sèvres vases (in less fearfully violent days, when the public could be trusted, the vases were displayed in the foyer of the Radio City Music Hall), but they are essentially local wine, sturdy but not to be tasted abroad. There is a man in J. D. Salinger's novel, *The Catcher in the Rye*, who keeps on saying of them: "You know what that is? That's precision," and there is not much more to be said.

They affirm sex and at the same time deny it. Their legs are a marvel and, all 72 of them, not at all conducive to erotic dreams. They say a great deal about New York and about American womanhood. That a human being can be turned into a machine, a dream not yet fully realized by American industrialists, is at least demonstrable in a form of minor art. That woman can be standardized in certain contexts is here certainly proved. That the perfection of American female beauty can be neutralized by multiplication is triumphantly shown every time they perform. One leaves the Radio City Music Hall feeling quite bemused and anxious to find real, imperfect women.

There are more real, imperfect women around in New York City than in California, where the long-stemmed, bronzed, toothy beauties are a triumph of conformity to a Central Casting blueprint. The mixture of races in New York is bizarre and produces remarkable kinds of comeliness. The

By night the ten-storey-high arches of the Metropolitan Opera House frame the warm glow emanating from its lobby. By day (below) they make a backdrop for Lincoln Center's spacious plaza. Seating 3,800, "the Met" is the largest of the Center's five main auditoriums.

girls do not rest smug in their beauty, as so many girls of the southern states seem to, but are made dynamic by the seething mix of bloods within them and by the city itself. They are sophisticated but not, like Parisian women, *blasées*; they are periodically tortured by self-doubt. Some of them are neurotic and have to go to psychiatrists. They have plenty to talk about. They will willingly drink with you in bars and talk.

I see I have been betrayed, or very nearly, into talking about women as a *pleasure*. No man would seriously object to being regarded as a *pleasure* by a woman, but women resent the sort of depersonalization, or Rocket-tization, it implies. (The Rockettes themselves presumably get over the problem by evoking principles of art: they are not a depersonalized femin-ine collective but a balletic mimesis of a fabulous machine.) But let me risk saying, before moving to less dangerous pleasures, that one of the finest of Manhattan pleasures to a man like myself is a long drinking session in a Third Avenue bar with a Manhattan girl, a walk with her through dangerous streets in intense winter cold, whatever intimacies are in order in her apart-ment or mine, a companionable viewing of the Late Late Date-with-the-Great Show over convalescent highballs. You may keep Central Park, the Museum of Modern Art and the poetry of William Cullen Bryant.

I propose now moving north to the Bronx, the original territory of the Dane, Johannes Bronck, home of the Bronx cheer and Yankee Stadium which resounds with it. In the stadium, apart from less secular activities which I shall come to later, two games may be played—baseball and football.

Football to the entire world, except for isolationist America, means soccer. American football looks like rugby in armour with heretical forward passing. Baseball is a tougher version of a game called rounders I used to play as a child in England. That both games mean much to Americans, and are a major pleasure of even New Yorkers, is attested by the size of Yankee Stadium, which can seat 54,000, and which requires more than 500 security men, gatekeepers and ushers and a squad of one hundred to clear up afterwards (a 14-hour job).

This stadium was built in 1923 to accommodate the Yankees—a baseball team which shares the loyalty of New Yorkers with the New York Mets. The greatest Yankee name of all time is that of Babe Ruth, who hit 60 home runs in the season of 1927—a record that stood until 1961 when, in a season longer by eight games, Roger Maris hit 61. Even in England, where we did not at the time know much about baseball (the American Army in Britain was later to work hard on our ignorance), the name Babe Ruth was known. He was mentioned in films and appeared in imported newsreels. His death was regarded as a national catastrophe and his obsequies were spectacular enough to be of international interest. He was laid out in the stadium, and a hundred thousand weeping fans came to do him homage.

He is commemorated here by a tombstone-like monument. Along with others honouring two similarly distinguished players, Lou Gehrig and Miller Huggins, it stands in an area of the stadium known as "Memorial Park", between the "bull pens" where pitchers warm up before entering the game—perhaps so that they may glance at it and be grateful Babe Ruth is not among the batters they will face. In this little pantheon there are also bronze plaques dedicated to other famous Yankee managers and players —Ed Barrow, Joe McCarthy, Mickey Mantle and Joe di Maggio, the latter once raised to a greater Valhalla through marriage to Marilyn Monroe ("I'm only an actress but Joe is one of the all-time greats."). And—is it baseball sharing religion's glory or vice versa?—there is a plaque commemorating Pope Paul's celebration of mass in Yankee Stadium in 1965.

The only fervour that can match that of sports fans is that of genuine religion. Religious bodies of varying kinds have organized rallies in Yankee Stadium. The Jehovah's Witnesses have been the best-liked clients because of their preternatural cleanliness. It is said that when a hundred thousand Witnesses assembled there, the 20,000 accommodated on the playing field itself wore no shoes so as not to damage the ground. They did their own cleaning up, and stadium folklore has it that when they were issued with 400 brooms for the purpose, they returned 440.

For my part, I prefer to visit the Bronx to see the zoo, finding this more elevating than either sport or religion. The Bronx Zoo is one of the finest in the world. It has a genuine, simulated African plain by the Bronx River, a bison range to cosset a threatened species, and enough comfort stations, as they are called, to remind one that civilization is not far away. As with Manhattan's Central Park, there is far too much to take in here, and I have always looked for misanthropic consolation in the larger mammals. In Samuel Butler's *The Way of All Flesh* an eminent London physician says:

"I have found the Zoological Gardens of service to many of my patients. I should prescribe for Mr. Pontifex a course of the larger mammals. Don't let him think he is taking them medicinally, but let him go to their house twice a week for a fortnight and stay with the hippopotamus, the rhinoceros and the elephants, till they begin to bore him. I find these beasts do my patients more good than any others. The monkeys are not a wide enough cross; they do not stimulate sufficiently. The larger carnivora are unsympathetic. The reptiles are worse than useless, and the marsupials are not much better; birds again, except parrots, are not very useful; he may look at them now and again, but with the elephants and the pig tribe generally he should mix just now as freely as possible."

The elephants of the Bronx Zoo are the finest relief imaginable after too many Bronx people. To see them dine is soothing medicine. They eat great piles of hay, whole loaves of bread and basketsful of cabbages and grain. Beside this, the ten-pound daily meal of the lion or tiger looks like an invalid regimen, what with its required cod liver oil and milk foods all mixed up in a "balanced meat diet" not unlike processed dog food. This is a remarkable zoo, overfacing in its variety (some 700 species, 2,800 individual beasts) and the Bronx matches it with a remarkable Botanical Garden—north of the zoo, beyond the Pelham Parkway.

It is evident, then, that short as my list is, New York City is not lacking the means of diversion. Sullen at the plethora of pleasure, far too many New Yorkers seek drug-induced inner space or the euphoria of drinking in gloomy bars. I have a fair knowledge of gloomy bars.

A Park for All Seasons

The southern half of Central Park confirms the prophetic vision of its designers, who foresaw its ultimate enclosure by "a continuous high wall of brick".

Central Park, created in the mid-19th Century as a marriage of nature and artifact, has been amazingly resilient during more than 100 years of harsh use. Topsoil—thousands of tons of which were added to enhance fertility—has been steadily eroded; half the 600 species of trees and shrubs have perished; rusting cans and old newspapers often clutter the paths; graffiti smear the surging whalebacks of rock; much of the grass is trodden to barrenness. Yet, the 840-acre rectangle remains a vibrant place, successfully serving Manhattan in a variety of roles: playground, wilderness, garden, theatre and gallery. From spring, when the first visiting birds wing in, to the return of the snows of winter it fulfils the purpose defined by its principal designer, Frederick Law Olmsted, in these words, " . . . to lift the mind out of the moods and habits of city life".

Paying by the half-hour, a time-watching customer gets an otherwise placid tour of the park in a hansom cab.

People, like these, who bike regularly in the park form friendships that transcend differences in age or fitness.

Spring: A Time of Quickening Life

As spring brings trees and shrubs into flower—early purple rhododendron blooms are soon followed by yellow forsythia and white magnolias—the park also blossoms with human activity. Picnicking parents fret over children scrambling on high, rocky outcrops. Droves of keep-fit joggers pound the paths. Migratory birds and spooning lovers make their seasonal appearances, and thousands of squirrels fatten on a new wealth of handouts.

On a springtime stroll a couple find crowds of daffodils, clouds of cherry blossom and room for an intimate talk—all rare commodities in the big city.

On a sultry day a couple pause by the Lake jammed with people in hired boats.

Summer Days of Heat and Action

The park, a venue for 24 officially listed sports and many
unofficial ones, is busiest in the hot city summer. Running
baseball players drum dust from worn grass. Others crowd in
to play tennis, sail model yachts, walk or simply loaf. On
evenings when the Philharmonic Orchestra plays in the park
100,000 may gather to hear its music in the dusk.

Stirring a haze of sunlit dust, strollers and cyclists throng the park on a warm evening. The bike in a tree (left) was put there for temporary safekeeping.

Runners and cyclists take advantage of the weekend ban on car traffic to time their speeds on the park roads.

Setting out a chamber-pot for contributions, a trio on violin, vibraphone and tuba fill the autumn air with music.

The Moods of Autumn

Autumn gives the park a touch of magic. In the sharp, chill air leaves turn yellow and then gold and flaming red (a transformation delayed by the protection of the surrounding buildings until two or three weeks after it happens in the suburban countryside). Cyclists— about 50,000 of them use the park on weekends—whiz through the gathering mists, and football players join the joggers, trampling the thickening carpet of fallen leaves.

Masses of colour-changing leaves, partly shaded from the sun by skyscrapers, make the park's eastern side seem a sea of vegetation washing on to Fifth Avenue.

Snow gives a fresh look to a familiar scene as sociable dog-owners monitor their pets' suspicious manoeuvres.

An exhilarated pair sled down a slope that has given winter pleasure to New York's children for over a century.

Winter Playground

In the first weeks of winter, the park, bare and bitter, attracts few people. But when hard frost and deep snows come, it is transformed again, its scars and litter hidden beneath a new white coat. Skaters glide on the lakes and pools, and sledding children swish down hillocks, reminding those who condemn the park for its declining condition that it still provides interludes of tranquillity for overwrought New Yorkers.

The modern city stands in dramatic contrast—as the park's designers intended—to a rural scene of snow-blanketed hills and outcrops of primeval rock.

9

Sure is a Busy Night

So much happens in and around New York, and it happens so fast, that New Yorkers sometimes feel they have been observers to all of history. For them time is telescoped; events pile on events with bewildering speed. In this concluding chapter, novelist Burgess offers the New Yorker's kaleidoscopic view of the recent past, as seen by the occupants of a mythical—though entirely possible—Manhattan drinking spot.—*The Editors.*

The man in the Third Avenue bar checked his watch with the clock over the shelves of bottles. 7.00 p.m., or 1900. He was thirsty, just having travelled down from the opening of the Bronx Zoo and, on the way south, been hindered in his passage by a great reception for the hero of the Spanish-American war, Admiral George Dewey. He ordered a cocktail invented only two minutes previously: a GNY (for Greater New York, a variation, naturally, of a Manhattan—whisky and vermouth, plus four olives).

At two minutes past the hour some workmen came in, sweating, dusty, triumphant, calling for beer. "Finished," one of them said.

"What's finished?" asked the man.

"The Flatiron Building. All 20 storeys. At Fifth Avenue and 23rd."

Before he could say more, there were cheers outside and the noise of a car braking. The barman said: "Made it then, all the way from San Francisco. First trans, trans—"

"Transcontinental?"

"That's it. Auto ride. Done it in 69 days."

A minute later a workman said: "Well, I can go home over the Williamsburg Bridge. Just finished." He checked with his watch. "First subway line should just about be ready too. Up Seventh Avenue. City Hall to West 145th."

"Surely," said our man, "you mean the Hudson Tubes to New Jersey?"

"That too?" The telephone on the bar-counter rang. The barman answered it and went white. He said:

"Oh my God. A thousand? *A thousand?* Oh, my God." And then: "Thank God, Thank God." He put the receiver down and said, chalk-white, to the customers: "Excursion. The *General Slocum.* On fire on the East River. Sunday school picnic. A thousand kids dead. *A thousand.* Thank God mine had a fever and stayed home."

It was too much to digest. They looked at one another, chalk-white, jaws dropped. A man, also chalk-white, smoking gun in his hand, dashed in and said: "Whisky. Large."

In the smoky atmosphere of a Manhattan bar, customers at the long counter thoughtfully sip their drinks and watch the passing parade.

"Yes, Mr. Thaw. Did you hear the—"

"I shot the bastard," said the man called Thaw. "Stanford White. Our greatest architect. Shot him on the roof of his own Madison Square Garden, damn him. Whisky. Large. That'll teach him to mess around with my wife. Another of those. Large." Two police officers were standing at the bar entrance. "Coming," said Thaw. "I'll go quietly. They'll make me plead insane, but I knew what I was doing. The bastard's dead." He left his gun on the counter in payment. The barman shook his head and nodded at a photograph stuck in the corner of the fly-blown mirror behind the bar.

"That's her," he said. "His wife, Evelyn Nesbit that was. Show girl, written all over her. Grrrr." He growled with desire. There was a rumbling under their feet. "That'll be it," he now said. "Subway between Manhattan and Brooklyn. Under the river." He looked at the clock. "Another minute and the Manhattan Bridge will be ready."

"And the Queensboro," said our man.

"Off," said one of the workmen, having drained his glass. "We'll just make the opening of Pennsylvania Station if we rush." He and his mates rushed. "Pardon me, lady," one of them said, almost bumping into a woman entering with a couple of books under her arm. The barman said:

"Here, lady." He handed her a small bottle of gin, for which she paid with pennies. "First there, right?" he said, nodding at the books.

She nodded a yes. "Beautiful library," she said, and left.

"New Public Library," the barman said. "Fifth and 42nd." Then, looking up into the clear air visible from the street window: "There he is, Mr. C. P. Rodgers in his airyplane. Off to Pasadena. First trans, trans—"

"Continental?"

"That's right. He'll never make it." He yawned and at once, down on Washington Place, 145 employees, most of them girls, died in a fire in the Triangle Shirtwaist Company's sweatshop. A minute after, although they would not know all the facts until a minute or two later, the *Titanic* struck an iceberg and began to go down. Fifteen hundred lost, including many prominent New Yorkers, not patrons of this bar. A snot-nosed urchin came in with evening papers and the barman took one. The urchin went out. Our man said: "I'll have another GNY."

The barman mixed it distractedly, looking at the front page. He said:

"Well, it's all out now. Police corruption. Cops with underworld connections. Police Lieutenant Charles Becker electrocuted for murdering the gambler Herman Rosenthal. A very nasty business." Giants marched past the door, off to their home at Coogan's Bluff, 155th Street. New York Giants, a baseball team. "Here, mister," said the bartender. And then: "God, the Mayor's dead."

"Bill Gaynor *dead*?"

"Shot, it says here, by discharged city employee. Is there no end to it all?" The clock still said only 1913. They could smell gunpowder coming from a distance. The new Grand Central Terminal opened. A street vendor looked in, bearing models of the Woolworth Building.

First transcontinental auto ride ends, 1903.

Evelyn Nesbit, pawn in crime of passion, 1906.

Workmen construct first
subway line, 1911.

"Souvenir, mister? World's biggest building, just finished."

"No thanks."

There was a three-minute silence. During it the sound of people shooting one another came nearer. "Foreigners," the bartender said. "Not human somehow. Not *American*. Frogs and Limeys and Krauts going bang bang at each other. Foreigners."

"We're all foreigners."

"Speak for yourself, mister," And then: "Krauts. Forty million bucks damage at Jersey City. Munitions ship blown up. Sabotage, I guess. Krauts. Got to kill the bastards. Can't stand the sausage-eating swine. Gotta go now, mister." He put on a military cap which he brought from under the counter. "You coming?"

"Wooden leg, see."

"Ah. George here will look after you." An aged man tottered in from the back room. "So long," saluted the other. He shambled off, mumbling "Over there, over there." In a minute he was back again. "Over there, over there," he said, throwing his cap all of five yards on to a peg. "Real tragedy on the subway. Near a hundred killed. Have to come back to the States to see the real slaughter."

The aged man, George, looked with insolent care at our man and said: "Gonna be some real bad news for you, mister. Better have another of them." He mixed him, shakily, another GNY.

"Bad news?" But our man's words were at once swallowed by a great noise from outside. The returned soldier ran to the peg for his cap and then ran to the door, crying: "Wait for me, General!"

Our man caught a glimpse of the returned Commander-in-Chief, General John J. Pershing, smiling, waving, borne aloft on the shoulders of

Triangle fire kills 145 workers, 1911.

Mayor Gaynor shot, 1910.

Babe Ruth, Home Run King, 1929.

weary, returned infantrymen. The procession passed, and a well-dressed man came in bearing a pile of press-wet newspapers. He said:

"I am Captain Joseph Medill Patterson. This is my brainchild. The *New York Daily News*. First with the latest. Look at that item. It's not happened yet." There was a faint boom downtown. "Ah yes, it has." The first page said: BOMB KILLS 33 AT HOUSE OF MORGAN. CHAOS AT BROAD AND WALL STREETS. WORK OF ANARCHISTS.

The bar began to fill very rapidly with desperately thirsty men. "What did I tell ya, mister?" said the old man, George, in triumph, drawing beer, glugging out whisky. The telephone rang and he went to it. He listened, nodded, put down the instrument, shouted: "Everybody out. We're closing up. That was Congressman Andrew J. Volstead. He's got Congress to bar liquor. Prohibition's coming in. You've got a minute to drink up."

Our man joined disgruntled crowds in the street. A drunken panhandler sang of the house that Ruth built. There was in the papers: the Yankee Stadium just built in the Bronx, a new home for the New York Yankees and their star, the greatest baseballer of all time, Babe Ruth. It was in Hearst's *Daily Mirror*, that minute on the streets.

Then it was in Bernarr Macfadden's *Graphic*, new that minute on the streets, shouting RAPE MURDER ADULTERY IN HIGH PLACES.

Funeral of Rudolph Valentino, 1926.

Our man stomped to Eighth and 50th. There were rejoicings at the completion of the new Madison Square Garden. But the rejoicings were speedily ousted by funeral music. The sky went black, the city was full of weeping women. The glass-topped coffin of Rudolph Valentino went by, surrounded by odorous lilies. Our man shook his head. Where could he go until the taverns opened up again? A scholarly-looking old gentleman came by, muttering to himself: "*Facile loqui, facile loqui.*" What did that mean? Our man had done some Latin in high-school. Speak easy? What did that mean? He followed, to a locked door, muttered his name through a tiny grille, gained admittance and found illicit liquor.

He emerged on to Wall Street to find it swathed in falling ticker-tape and full of cheering from windows. A man with a megaphone was announcing: "Here they come now—the intrepid Lieutenant Commander soon to be Admiral Richard E. Byrd and Floyd Bennett, fresh from their flight, the first ever over the North Pole. Here she comes now—New York's own Gertrude Ederle, first woman ever to swim the English Channel. There they go. And now and now and now—"

He was drowned by the screaming of ecstatic voices. He checked his watch: 1927. The ticker tape was like an Egyptian plague of tapeworms. "Here he is, here he is, the great, the intrepid, the heroic Charles A. Lindbergh, first man ever to fly solo from New York to Paris. This service comes to you by courtesy of the Roxy Theater, world's largest, just open at Seventh Avenue and 50th. See a chorus of thousands perform the new sensation, the Lindy Hop."

But our man was much more interested in going to see the first great talkie, *The Jazz Singer*, with Al Jolson. It was not all talking and singing, but

Wall Street Crash, 1929.

Lindbergh ticker-tape parade, 1927.

Repeal of Prohibition, 1933.

enough to make a revolution in movie history. No more silents. After it the cinema manager came on to the stage to say: "News has just come through of the execution of Judd Gray and Ruth Snyder for the foul crime of the murder of the latter's husband. Stay in your seats, folks—more to come."

Wearily our man stomped out to find ambulances and stretchers and screams in Times Square—18 killed in subway wreck. He looked wearily up to see the *Graf Zeppelin* airship high in the heavens, ready to be moored at Lakehurst, New Jersey, after the first commercial transatlantic flight. The newsboys were screaming: "Read all about it, notorious gambler Arnold Rothstein shot in Park Central Hotel, read all about it."

And then and then and then. O stars hide your lights, O sun be quenched, O moon go into mourning. Our man, in a speakeasy, heard the crash, like the falling of all the towers of all the cities of all the world. The Wall Street disaster (it was on the radio). Sixteen million shares sold. Drinkers in the speakeasy, hearing the news, shot themselves and one another. Our man emerged into the street to see the completion of the Chrysler Building, world's tallest. Men stood ready to leap out of the windows. "Don't jump," he shouted. They didn't, for already someone walking in the gutter was singing to a banjo: "Happy days are here again. . . ."

Happy days. Our man painfully stomped to where the Empire State Building, world's tallest, had been completed. It was 1931. A man, eyes on his watch, not on the soaring tower, was saying:

"One minute to go, fifty-five, fifty—" The scholarly old gentleman had reappeared, muttering:

"*Non facile loqui, non facile loqui.*"

Our man understood. No more speakeasies. Repeal of Prohibition. He took a cab to his old Third Avenue haunt. The cab-driver said: "All crooks. Mayor Walker, accused of graft. Gentleman Jim they call him, now he has to resign. Walker walks."

"This is not the way."

"Sure it's not the way. Thought you'd like to see that, see—Radio City Music Hall. To cheer everybody up and make 'em forget all about municipal corruption. Okay, now we go to where you wanta go, if I can get through that crowd there parading their support of Roosevelt and his New Deal. Ah, I see we got ourselves a new Mayor."

Fiorello H. La Guardia waved from an open car; next to him sat, very sour-faced, District Attorney Thomas E. Dewey, papers on his knees, all ready to bust rackets. Our man reached his Third Avenue bar.

There was a new barman. "Yeah, bud?" he said.

Our man asked for a new cocktail, an MBQ. After all, the Triborough Bridge had just opened, linking the three boroughs, Manhattan, the Bronx and Queens. There was an excitable Frenchman saying: "*Le plus grand navire du monde. Et le plus vite. Vive la Normandie.*" He drank off something straw-coloured.

An old man said to our man: "Just come in on that big ship. Frog, he is. Speaks Frog. World's biggest, he says."

"He's wrong, old boy," said an English voice. "*I've* just come in on the *Queen Mary*. That's the world's biggest." A florid man nodded in self-satisfaction of a referred kind and ordered beer. He drank and, with frothy lips, said: "The only way to cross. You hear what just this minute happened in New Jersey? At that dirigible landing field—what's it called?"

"Lakehurst?" said our man.

"That's right. The *Hindenburg* burnt up soon as it landed. Thirty six dead. Big crowds rushing to see the wreckage via the Lincoln Tunnel. Just opened you know."

The bartender turned on the radio. The voice of Douglas Corrigan came through crackling static, all the way from Dublin. He had just flown from Brooklyn, solo, but without flying permit. He was hotly denying that he had done anything wrong. "I guess I flew the wrong way," he kept saying.

"Only way to cross," said the florid Englishman. Over the radio came a new sound—that of the Sixth Avenue El being dismantled. "Well, must be on my way. Got to go to Boston. Got to get a cab to La Guardia."

"What you wanta see our Mayor for?" asked the old man.

"Mayor? Said nothing about a Mayor. La Guardia, I said. That's an airport, just opened."

"I'll share a cab with you," said a thin-faced Yankee. "Drop me at the New York World's Fair, Flushing Meadow Park, Queens. I hear your King George and Queen Mary are coming to see it. We'll show your anachronistic monarch a thing or two."

"Get your own cab," the Englishman said. He had been listening attentively to the radio. "I'm on my way home. War's just broken out." He left. The barman said to everybody:

"Foreigners going bang bang at each other. Krauts and Limeys and Frogs. Polacks and Bohunks. Foreigners."

"We're all foreigners," said our man.

"You speak for yourself bud."

The Frenchman had left just before the Englishman. The bar contained only Americans. They heard a distant rumble. "Guns," said the barman. But it was traffic in the Queens–Midtown Tunnel under the East River, just opened. An Englishman came in, wearing naval uniform. He ordered beer. "You should be fighting that darned war of yours," said the barman. The Englishman said:

"I *am* fighting it. Just came in on the *Queen Elizabeth*, world's largest."

"Why?" asked our man.

"Secret mission, old boy."

"Christ," said the bartender. "Them foreigners is going to drag us into it. Secret mission, he says." At that moment the lights went out all over New York. "What did I say?" said the barman.

"Yeah, we're in it, I guess," a drinker said. "It's the Japs. Dirty little fighters." The Frenchman who had been there before, now came back again, weeping, babbling.

"What's he say?" asked the old man. "I don't understand Frog talk."

Radio City Music Hall opens, 1932.

Bomber crashes into Empire State Building, 1945.

Completion of La Guardia Airport, 1939.

SS Normandie, capsized in the Hudson, 1942.

"The *Normandie*," said our man. "Burned and capsized in the Hudson."

"Well," said the bartender. "I guess it's me off to play soldiers. Old George'll look after ya." The old man who had been there before came in again, nodding maliciously at our man. A well-dressed thug, unshaven, gun pointing, entered, saying:

"Don't nobody move."

"Why," said old George, "If it ain't 'Lepke' Buchalter. Killed more men than you've ate hot dinners." He said to our man: "Runs what they calls Murder Incorporated in Brooklyn. What'll it be, 'Lepke'?"

"Don't nobody move. First guy moves I pumps him fulla lead."

"All right, drop it," said a voice. Louis 'Lepke' Buchalter turned, ready to fire. He thought better of it. A cop took his gun. A portly police lieutenant said: "You're coming with us."

"I ain't done nothin' wrong. Here all the time, wasn't I, fellers?"

"You're going to fry, and soon too," said the lieutenant. "We know all about who pushed Abe 'Kid Twist' Reles from the window of the Half Moon Motel on Coney Island."

"The cops done it. Under police protection, wozny?"

"We know the lot, 'Lepke'. The lot, all of it. Come on, let's go."

"I wanna speak to my lawyer."

"Plenty of time for that at headquarters."

There was a silence, broken into by odd spurts of war news. There was a loud bang, all the way from Hiroshima. "Reckon that's about it, then," said old George. There was a victory procession outside. Everybody yawned. A man entered to install a television set. He switched it on and a handsome, greying announcer gave the news. "New York," he said, "has been selected as permanent headquarters for the United Nations. Meetings will be held at Hunter College, Flushing Meadow Park and Lake Success, Long Island, pending the building of a permanent UN Headquarters on First Avenue facing the East River. It is announced that—" A telephone rang on his desk. "Pardon me," he said, answering it. And then, putting it down, gravely: "An Army plane has just hit the seventy-ninth floor of the

Empire State Building. Fourteen persons are reported killed. To resume. It is announced that John D. Rockefeller Junior has—" The telephone rang again. "Pardon me." Gravely he said: "An Army plane has just hit the fifty-eighth floor of the Bank of Manhattan Building with the loss of five lives. To resume. John D. Rockefeller Junior has donated land to the United Nations for the construction of a headquarters building."

"Turn it off," said a man with a twitch. "The place's crawling with foreigners. Krauts and Nips and all. Looks like it's snowing," he said, looking at the window.

It was. 25.8 inches fell, breaking the record set by the blizzard of 1888 about an hour previously. It cleared up. The sun shone. Our man nodded and left. On the street he saw an airline bus going to the newly opened Idlewild International Airport. "Won't keep that name for long," he said to himself. He took a cab to the Federal Courthouse for the trial of 11 leaders of the U.S. Communist Party on charges of conspiracy to overthrow the government. He heard Alger Hiss convicted of perjury. He left and decided to have a haircut.

On the way to the barbershop he favoured he heard that there had been two crashes on the Long Island railroad, with 111 deaths. He yawned. The Brooklyn Battery Tunnel was opened. He yawned. He saw people running to see the SS *United States*, America's largest ship, sail off on her maiden voyage to break the transatlantic speed record. Hurricane Hazel blew at 113 miles an hour and then blew herself out like a candle. Serge Rubinstein, financial wizard, was mysteriously murdered. Our man yawned. Busloads of shipwreck survivors appeared in Manhattan. "What happened?" our man asked a telephone repairman.

"Dat Eyetalian ship de *Andrea Doria* cracked into dat Swede ship de *Stockholm* off Nantucket Island. De *Ile de France* brought da lot in."

A man ran by screaming, blinded by acid. Racketeers got into a car, grinning. So much for Victor Riesel, famous *New York Mirror* labour columnist, exposer of rackets. Our man entered the barbershop and sat wearily down. He yawned. The barber, wrapping him in white, nodded in the direction of a swarthy customer being massaged around his round jowls.

"That," he said, "is Albert Anastasia."

At that moment a man with a mad face entered, home-made bomb in hand. He was immediately followed by two cops, who arrested him, searched him for further bombs, then took him away.

"So much for the Mad Bomber," the barber said, snipping at the back of our man. "At it since 1940 and the time now is 1957. Planted them bombs everywhere. Twenty-two went off. There sure are some mad guys in this world."

The cool, moist peace of the barbershop erupted into violent life, or death. Men came in with guns and killed Albert Anastasia. He died very surprised in a white shroud. "Sure are some mad guys in this world," said the barber. And, to an assistant, "Clear that chair there for the next

Long Island railroad crash, 1950.

Barbershop murder of Albert Anastasia, 1957.

Alger Hiss tried for perjury, 1950.

SS United States' maiden voyage, 1952.

customer." While our man was trimmed an aeroplane taking off from La Guardia crashed into the East River, killing 65. Two aeroplanes collided over the city, one falling in Brooklyn, the other in Staten Island, with a loss of 134 lives. An airliner crashed into Jamaica Bay after taking off from Idlewild, 94 dead. Our man left the barbershop ready to greet Lieutenant Colonel John H. Glenn Jr., first American to orbit the earth. But there were many around unwilling to be jubilant about this national achievement.

"See that? Worst day on Wall Street since the crash."

"Seen this? New York Mets? Talk about disasters. One hundred and twenty games lost, one hun—"

There was loud acclaim for Gordon Cooper, who had also orbited the earth. In the Philharmonic Hall, the first segment of Lincoln Center for the Performing Arts to be completed, Leonard Bernstein was conducting the New York Philharmonic. The Pan Am Building had opened, biggest in the city in terms of floor space. The endless newspaper strike had ended. The *New York Mirror* knew it could not recover, however. One hundred and ninety million dollars lost in business to the city. Jesus.

In Dallas, John F. Kennedy was assassinated by Lee Harvey Oswald. The shock. New York was hushed but violent. Our man went back to his Third Avenue bar. There had been a change of bartender.

"What'll it be, friend?"

"A GNY." He looked at his watch. "Plenty sure happens here in a short time."

"You can say that again, friend. Here you are. One GNY cocktail straight up with four olives. Plenty sure does happen here, all right. And we ain't hardly started yet."

Mad Bomber arrested, 1957.

High and Mighty

PHOTOGRAPHS BY JAY MAISEL

The flat tops and steep sides of new skyscrapers lining the Avenue of the Americas—Sixth Avenue to New Yorkers—cut a patch of sky into opposing arrows.

The stroller in New York glimpses the sky as a series of zigzag shapes carved by the sharp edges of the surrounding buildings, dazzling and arrestingly beautiful patterns of light and shadow that often were not conceived by a single architect but emerged spontaneously with the city's upward growth. A head-craning view can be exhilarating—even disorienting—as sunlight and its reflection pour down the sides of glass walls in shimmering waves. To capture this dizzying Manhattan, photographer Jay Maisel walked its deeps and, aiming his camera skywards—sometimes straight up, as in the photograph above—produced images that stand the city on end. The power that seems to stream from the buildings is one of the qualities that has made New York a wonder of the modern world—its only true 20th-Century metropolis.

The sloping glass façade of "9" West 57th Street, built in 1973, picks up both the image and the shadow of an older skyscraper on the corner of Fifth Avenue.

One of the 110-storey towers of the World Trade Center slices a chunk out of its twin with its shadow.

The stepped floors of an aluminium skyscraper contrast with the austere back of a Fifth Avenue neighbour.

The curved side of the Americana Hotel on Seventh Avenue sweeps towards another building, giving the illusion that its foreshortened wall bends into a column.

One gleaming Park Avenue structure seems to dissolve the front of another.

Windows reflecting windows near 57th Street weave a sedate urban plaid.

Appearance and reality merge in the corner of a court in a mid-Manhattan building as light and shadows criss-cross surfaces and throw back overlapping images.

A midtown skyscraper's shimmering wall of glass reflects mundane buildings across the way and turns them into a multitude of topsy-turvy fantasy structures.

Bibliography

Asbury, Herbert, *Gangs of New York.* Alfred A. Knopf, New York, 1928.
Ashton, Dore, *New York.* World Cultural Guide, Thames and Hudson, London, 1974.
Bliven, Bruce Jr., *Battle for Manhattan.* Penguin Books, Baltimore, 1964.
Callow, Alexander B. Jr., *The Tweed Ring.* Oxford University Press, New York, 1966.
Campbell, Alexander, *The Trouble with Americans.* Rupert Hart-Davis, London, 1971.
Clarke, John Henrik, *Harlem, U.S.A.* Collier Books, New York, 1971.
Conrad, Earl, *Billy Rose: Manhattan Primitive.* World Publishing Co., Cleveland, 1968.
Costikyan, Edward N., *Behind Closed Doors: Politics in the Public Interest.* Harcourt Brace Jovanovich, London, 1968.
Ellison, Ralph, *Invisible Man.* Penguin Books.
Ertz, Susan, *New York Panorama.* Constable, London, 1939.
Glazier, Nathan, and Moynihan, Daniel Patrick, *Beyond the Melting Pot.* The M.I.T. Press, London, 1970.

Harrington, Michael, *The Other America: Poverty in the United States.* Macmillan Publishing Co., New Jersey, 1970.
Jacobs, Jane, *The Death and Life of Great American Cities.* Jonathan Cape, London, 1962.
Jones, Howard, *Crime in a Changing Society.* Penguin Books, Baltimore, 1965.
Kaufmann, Edgar Jr., *The Rise of an American Architecture.* Pall Mall Press, London, 1970.
Klein, Alexander, *The Empire City.* Rhinehart & Co., New York, 1955.
Lewis, Oscar, *La Vida: A Puerto Rican Family in the Culture of Poverty.* Random House, Maryland, 1966.
Michelin, *Green Guide to New York City.* France, 1974.
Mills, C. Wright, *Power, Politics and People: Collected Essays.* Oxford University Press, New York, 1968.
Moore, Harry T., *Henry James and his World.* Thames and Hudson, London, 1974.
Morris, James, *The Great Port.* Faber and

Faber, London, 1970.
Passos, John Dos, *United States of America.* Penguin Books, 1966.
Rimanelli, Giose, *Tragica America.* Immordino, Genova, 1968.
Riordan, William, *Plunkitt of Tammany Hall.* Dutton E. P., & Co., New York, 1946.
Robotti, Frances Diane, *Key to New York: Empire City.* Fountainhead, New York, 1964.
Roth, Henry, *Call it Sleep.* Avon Books, New York, 1974.
Sayre, Wallace S., and Kaufman, Herbert, *Governing New York City.* Norton, W. W. & Co., New York, 1965.
Still, Bayrd, *Mirror for Gotham.* New York University Press, 1956.
Toffler, Alvin, *Future Shock.* Pan Books, London, 1973.
Wagner, Geoffrey, *Another America: In Search of Canyons.* Allen & Unwin, London, 1972.
Wheeler, Thomas C. (ed), *Immigrant Experience: The Anguish of Becoming American.* Penguin Books, Maryland, 1972.

Picture Credits

Index

Numerals in italics indicate a photograph or drawing of the subject mentioned

Colour reproduction by Irwin Photography Ltd., at their Leeds PDI Scanner Studio.
Filmsetting by C. E. Dawkins (Typesetters) Ltd., London, SE1 1UN.
Printed and bound in Italy by Arnoldo Mondadori, Verona.